The Family, Communes, and Utopian Societies

Edited by Sallie TeSelle

HARPER TORCHBOOKS ❦
Harper & Row, Publishers
New York, Evanston, San Francisco, London

This work was originally published in the Spring 1972 issue of
Soundings.

First TORCHBOOK edition published 1972.

LIBRARY OF CONGRESS CATALOG CARD NUMBER: 72–7853

STANDARD BOOK NUMBER: 06–131741–1

CONTENTS

The editorial policy of *Soundings* is to "highlight those insights, findings, and issues in diverse fields of study which disclose serious humane concerns." Since the concern with alternative life styles today is one such "serious humane concern," we decided to sponsor a working seminar in an attempt to engage the problem in an interdisciplinary way.* It was an exciting time. The "experts" found themselves in new territory, working "out of" disciplines but toward goals that were novel for them both personally and professionally: a philosopher spoke about his experience in an urban commune, a theologian depicted his dream of a rural homestead, a journalist wrote about day care. There were no prima donnas in this seminar, for the options were new, the directions many. What happened was that rare phenomenon of scholars seeing themselves as learners; since no one "knew the answer," every idea was viewed as a possible direction rather than as a criticism of someone's pet thesis. What emerged is the present set of papers, published originally as a special issue of *Soundings* (Spring 1972).

It is not and could not be a thematically unified set of essays. Yet a theme of sorts emerges, a theme which is a central and very old one to the American experience, set out in John McDermott's opening essay. It is the complex dialectic between the city and the country, the ambivalent attitude toward the city which Mc-Dermott calls "nature nostalgia" and which he claims no longer serves well the American people, who now are urban. The dialectic is picked up in Kirk Jeffrey's study of the nineteenth-century family's retreat to the country in its search for utopia. In less direct ways the urban side of American life is affirmed in the Ogilvys'

---

* The seminar was held at the annual conference of the Society for Religion in Higher Education, August 1971, at Wells College, Aurora, New York.

piece on communes and in the Steinfels' article on day care; the countryside is touched on in Kaufman's essay on the homesteading movement, Sturm's on the kibbutzim, and Garrett's on Coleridge's utopia. Another way to suggest the thematic unity of the pieces is through the play on the words utopia and eutopia, reality and realization that occurs so frequently in the titles. The dialectic of reality and utopia, of city and country, is, in complex ways, *the* American dialectic. It is the naive dream of our fathers and mothers who saw America as the land of an innocent Adam, pristine and pure; it is also the more sober dream of all who still hope in America, believing that its survival depends, not on escaping the harsh realities of the city, but on bringing to bear upon those realities the idealism and utopianism that has too often been a mechanism of escape rather than of renewal. We offer this set of papers as a contribution to that ongoing conversation on the American dream: the dream that life in this land can be good, not for the few, but for all who call it home.

S. T.S.

NATURE NOSTALGIA AND THE CITY:

An American Dilemma

JOHN J. McDERMOTT

> ... that men shall say of succeeding plantacions: the lord make it like that of New England: for we must Consider that wee shall be as a Citty upon a Hill, the eies of all people are uppon us; ...
>
> John Winthrop

> The only room in Boston which I visit with alacrity is the Gentlemen's Room at the Fitchburg Depot, where I wait for cars sometimes for two hours, in order to get out of town.
>
> Thoreau

GENERALIZATIONS about national cultures are not notoriously inexact, for exceptions abound. The judgments of a single perceiver, however imaginative, are often narrowing. This is especially true of interpretations of a culture as vast and as complex as America. Nonetheless, cultures often subsequently live out these generalizations, for they are frequently articulations of deeply held images, projected onto the stream of history. In many instances, whatever the paucity of facts at the origin of the generalization, its power soon engenders the sustaining empirical support.[1] So true is this of analyses of American culture that one recent commentator, Daniel Boorstin, can hold that we live in terms of "pseudo-events,"[2] make-ups which take their place in our consciousness as reality.

Despite the methodological problems[3] and the warning of Boorstin, and while not oblivious to the risk of self-deception, I offer that the following generalization has uncommonly profound

Mr. McDermott teaches urban aesthetics, American philosophy, and philosophy of culture at Queens College, CUNY. He is the editor of comprehensive editions of the writings of William James and Josiah Royce and has published articles on aesthetics and contemporary culture.

1

and expansive empirical roots: American urban man has been seduced by nature. By this I mean that at the deepest level of his consciousness urban man functions on behalf of nature metaphors, nature expectancies, and a nostalgia for an experience of nature which neither he nor his forbears actually underwent. For contemporary America, the implications of this situation are significant. In the first place, we are blocked off from understanding the dramatic and necessary conflict with nature, which characterized American life until recently. Indeed, we have become naive and ahistorically sentimental about that conflict. Second, we have often failed to diagnose the limitations and strengths of our present urban context on its own terms, rather than as a function of the absence of nature.

I am not, of course, claiming that this contention about the role of nature is the only or even the major key to the solution of the American urban crisis. On the other hand, I do hold that much contemporary diagnosis, whether of ecology, youth culture or alienation, is woefully out of context without some grasp of the significance of this theme in the development of American consciousness. The basic problem is not one of general inattention, for we have a rich and long-standing literature on the meaning of nature and, of more recent vintage, an escalating literature on the city. We do not, however, have a broad tradition of analysis which focuses on their interrelationship, especially as written from the side of the urban experience. So as not to be waylaid by the vastness of our theme, let us consider the fundamental meaning of nature in American culture and its import for our understanding of time and the related possibilities for institutional transformation. If we then contrast this analysis with similar themes at work in urban consciousness, we should have some insight to the subtle but powerful role of nature in our present urban difficulties.

NATURE AS CONTEXT

For it is the wilderness that is the mother of that nation, it was in the wilderness that the strange and lonely people who have not yet spoken but who inhabit that immense and terrible land from East to West, first knew themselves, it was in the living wilderness that they faced one another at ten paces and shot one another down, and it is in the wilderness that they still live.

—Thomas Wolfe, *Men of Old Catawba*

Even the slightest familiarity with the history of American culture, especially its literary stand, will yield an awareness of the extraordinary importance of the nature motif. The philosophical dimensions of the meaning of nature are deeply rooted in European thought, beginning with the notion of *phusis* in Greek culture and reconstituted subsequently as *natura* in medieval and early modern philosophy. The complexities of the development of this notion are endless, as an analysis of that aspect called "natural law" will readily reveal. This tradition does not account, however, for the meaning of nature in American culture.

In America there was an originating clarity to the experience and understanding of nature; it meant land, ferocious but untrammeled and free. The experience of nature in the early history of American culture was set in a dialectical tension between wilderness and paradise, or perhaps more accurately, a dialectic *inside* wilderness between desert and garden, between terror and salvation.[4] The odyssey of the Puritan is instructive in this regard. The Puritan had a profound sense of unregeneracy built into the very fabric of his being, as if the struggle between wilderness and paradise were being played out within his own autobiography.[5] On the American scene, the Puritan confronted wilderness as an external phenomenon, and its presence within his own soul slowly became eroded. In time, American man saw himself, his very presence, as the salvific factor in an unregenerate wilderness; paradise as the planting of a garden in the wild. Change these terms to the language of the expanding frontier and you have an intriguing insight into the American drive to conquer nature.[6]

From the time of the Puritans to the beginning of our century, despite vast geographical differentiae, nature experienced as land was held to be the fundamental locus for symbolic formulations of our cultural and religious life. The struggle for survival in a physical sense was undoubtedly an irreducible matrix in this confrontation with the land. Morton and Lucia White write that "land ruled supreme, and seemingly limitless untamed nature, rather than the city, was the gigantic obstacle that confronted the five million people who populated the United States of America in 1800."[7] Beginning with the Puritans, however, there was another and deeper sense of that obstacle: one which saw the land as nothing less than the New Jerusalem. For the Puritans, if the kingdom is to come, it will come upon the land and show itself as continuous with the rhythms of nature. At the close of a moving paragraph on the correspondence of nature to salvation, Samuel Sewall writes in his "Phaenomena" (1697):

> As long as nature shall not grow old and dote but shall constantly remember to give the rows of Indian Corn their education, by Pairs: So long shall Christians be born there; and being first made meet, shall from thence be Translated, to be made partakers of the Inheritance of the Saints in Light.[8]

The role of nature in personal regeneration becomes tremendously intensified on the American scene. It is a dominant theme in the life and conversion experiences of Jonathan Edwards, for whom the "doctrines of the gospel" were to his soul as "green pastures."[9] And in the nineteenth-century revisiting of the paradise theme, we witness the harrowing journey of the Mormons from Nauvoo, Illinois to the Great Salt Lake as quest for salvation, "a stake in Zion," played out against the backdrop of an alternating violence and beneficence of the land. In 1835, James Brooks sees Nature as the guarantor of our salvation.

> God has promised us a renowned existence, if we will but deserve it. He speaks this promise in the sublimity of Nature. It resounds all along the crags of the Alleghanies. It is uttered in the thunder of Niagara. It is heard in the war of two oceans, from the great Pacific to the rocky ramparts of the Bay of Fundy. . . The august TEMPLE in which we dwell was built for lofty purposes. Oh! that we may consecrate it to LIBERTY and CONCORD, and be found fit worshippers within its holy wall.[10]

In commenting on this and similar assertions, Perry Miller writes: "so then—because America, beyond all nations, is in perpetual touch with Nature, it need not fear the debauchery of the artificial, the urban, the civilized." And, he adds, that nature "had effectually taken the place of the Bible."[11] Closer to our time, at the beginning of this century, John Muir, under the rubric of conservationist language, sees salvation as tied to the preservation of wilderness and the American struggle as one "between landscape righteousness and the Devil."[12] Muir had also written that "thousands of nerve-shaken, over-civilized people are beginning to find out that going to the mountains is going home; that wildness is a necessity; and that mountain parks and reservations are useful not only as fountains of timber and irrigating rivers, but as fountains of life."[13]

The messianic interpretation of the land was not always cast in biblical or even religious language. In a parallel development, the history of American thought also brought forth a tradition which understood the land as an ethical and political resource able to transform human nature for the better. Nowhere is this more obvious than in the early writings of Thomas Jefferson. In his *Notes on the State of Virginia,* Jefferson offers that "those who labor in the earth are the chosen people of God . . . While we have land to labor then, let us never wish to see our citizens occupied at a work bench, or twirling a distaff." [14] Jefferson sees the workshop as associated with cities, and it is thereby better to have them remain in Europe, for "the mobs of great cities add just so much to the support of pure government as sores do to the strength of the human body. It is the manners and spirit of a people which preserve a republic in vigor. A degeneracy in these is a canker which soon eats to the heart of its laws and constitution." [15]

In a strain anticipatory of much of later American thought, [16] Jefferson sees the commitment to the land as passionate and moral. John Anderson, in his book on *The Individual and the New World,* writes that

> Jefferson found in his American experience a faith that man's egoism might disappear under some conditions of human commitment to the new land.
>
> In his conception that man's commitment to the New World might contain the principle for the control of man's natural egoism, Jefferson not only re-directed attention to the environment of the American continent, he suggested that man's true nature emerged from this reference. Jefferson sought thus to formulate those conditions of human acceptance of the New World under which man's moral nature might emerge and effectively control his egoism. [17]

The experience of the land as a basis for a democratic ethos, as articulated by Jefferson, remained a deep characteristic of American political literature throughout the nineteenth century, but it did not negate completely the earlier biblical dimension which saw the land as the readiness for the coming of the kingdom in time. The convergence of these attitudes toward the land are found not only in the evangelical interpretation of frontier experience but in the symbolic versions of man's place in nature as found in Emerson and Thoreau. Writing in 1927, Lucy Lockwood

Hazard in her book on *The American Frontier and American Literature* stated that "it is time to strip from the Emersonian hero the decorous toga and conventional mask with which rhetoric and philosophy have disguised him, and show that 'the American Scholar' and Davy Crockett are brothers . . . "[18] It was, after all, in the address on "The American Scholar" that Emerson told us "so much only of life as I know by experience, so much of the wilderness have I vanquished and planted, or so far have I extended my being, my dominion."[19]

Emerson has a deep feeling for what Leo Marx refers to as the "metaphysical powers of landscape."[20] And this sensibility lends him to an abiding hostility against the city. In his essay on "Culture" Emerson writes,

> Whilst we want cities as the centres where the best things are found, cities degrade us by magnifying trifles, the country man finds the town a chop-house, a barber's shop. He has lost the lines of grandeur of the horizon hills and plains, and with them sobriety and elevation. He has come among a supple, glib-tongued tribe, who live for show, servile to public opinion. Life is dragged down to a fracas of pitiful cares and disasters. You say the Gods ought to respect a life whose objects are their own; but in cities they have betrayed you to a cloud of insignificant annoyances.[21]

In a note to that text, Emerson is cited as having commented that on his passing the woods on Walden Ledge, "on the way to the city, how they reproach me!"[22] The land, then, was more than open space and sylvan woods; it was a spiritual resource and a moral challenge. Thoreau offers us the most perceptive phrasing of this power of the land:

> All things invite this earth's inhabitants
> To rear their lives to an unheard of height
> And meet the expectation of the land: . . . [23]

It is the "expectation of the land" which has driven us notwithstanding to repeated disappointments in the realization of these expectations. In Perry Miller's phrase, we are "nature's nation."[24] And for John Anderson, our visions about the possibility of the land "express an intuition of the reflexive direction of human energy necessary to freedom. In such intuitions, Americans have seen themselves as marching across the wilderness and with more or less clarity have conceived of themselves as representative of mankind's ultimate place in the

unknown universe." [25] The empirical basis for these mythic
interpolations of our experiencing the land was the sheer
prodigality of space and the related reconstituting of our
experience of time. The importance of this interrelationship of
space and time within the context of our experience of nature
cannot be overestimated, for the experience of time is a crucially
distinctive characteristic of any culture, and as we replaced nature
experience with urban experience we failed to re-orient our sense
of space and time in a way consistent with this shift in context.

In specific terms, the experience of nature as open and free
space generated for Americans a sense of time as option, as
possibility. In an essay on "The American People: Their Space,
Time and Religion," Sidney Mead comments that

> Americans never had time to spare. What they did have during all their
> formative years was space—organic, pragmatic space—the space of action.
> And perhaps this made the real difference in the formation of "this new
> man." [26]

Space, however, is time undergone. The absence of "time to
spare" really means the absence of time as introverted experience,
that is, the absence of the struggle to achieve identity while
subject to the contours of fixed options. Spatial claustrophobia
turns us in on ourselves, interiorizing the landscape so that it is
continuous with our imagination rather than with our vision. Over
against this, in a context of open space, there is the possibility of
projecting oneself outward and achieving identity as subject to the
emerging novelties of the space of action. The presence of options
gave dignity to events, for they were chosen rather than inherited.
Put otherwise, a man could come to himself by relocating. The
"space of action" was the locus of novelty and, paradoxically, the
locus of self-awareness. Growth was inseparable from shifts in
spatial contours, thereby indirectly transforming our experience of
time from that of waiting, backing and filling, to that of
anticipating and the structuring of possibility. The shift in the
word "trip" is instructive here, for its present meaning of a
hallucinogenic visit to our inner landscape contrasts starkly with
its open-ended spatial exploration in the vernacular of nature
language. [27] Nature experienced as open space was not a nature in
which man sat, derivative and self-preening. On the contrary, the
undergoing of nature of which I speak found man grappling and
reaching, fed always by shifts in location, even when such shifts
came to him vicariously, as in the influence of the legendary

evocations of the "mountain men" on the consciousness of the Eastern seaboard. [28]

It is important to realize that the space of which I speak was riddled with drama, not only of natural origins—mountains, forests, and great rivers—but of socio-political origin—the presence of Indians and the struggles over territory and gold. Space, flat and boxed, is not a sufficiently humanizing context for man's situation. The drama of space is proportionate to its capacity for novelty. In the experience of nature, movement is necessary whether it be real or vicarious, the assumption being that something new, different, better is out there, just over the next ridge. In that tradition we are riven with the need of beginning again and again. Commenting on Emerson's oracular text, "why should not we also enjoy an original relation to the universe?" [29] Frederick Jackson Turner asks, "Let us believe in the eternal genesis, the freshness and value of things present, act as though, just created, we stood looking a new world in the face and investigate for ourselves and act regardless of past ideas." [30] It is this quest for novelty, expressed while he was still a young man, that we should read into Turner's later designation of the meaning of American space as a frontier, namely, as a series of options.

When events are framed against novel occurences, the experience of ordinary living takes on the hue of an imaginative reconstruction of life. William James, for example, has written that "according to my view, experience as a whole is a process in time . . . " [31] But if the setting for this process, relative to each life lived, is characterized by repetition and by the plodding dullness of a context that rarely, if ever, is broken into by basic shifts in direction and possibility, then however eschatologically viable, our lives experience little of import in immediate terms. [32] The sense of option, as created by the novelties of open space, enabled American man to ground a deeply felt but rarely sustained religious belief, namely that the passing of time was a healing and liberating experience.

By way of specifying this contention, let us take as example from one of America's most profound although unappreciated philosophers, Josiah Royce. A Californian and a child of the frontier, Royce was born in the mining camp of Grass Valley, high in the Sierras. His early experience bequeathed to him a fascination with the evolution of American communities, especially their combination of moral imagination and novel physical settings. Royce believed that landscape and climate were constitutive of consciousness, and given man's efforts time was a healing force. In his *History of California*, Royce describes the evolution of a mining community in a section he entitles "The Struggle for Order: Self-Government, Good Humor and Violence in the Mines." Royce's conclusion to this chapter illustrates the earlier commitment to a salvific future as witnessed and sustained by the possibilities inherent in an open and fecund nature (though the last line of this text is depressing, for, as we too well know, rivers no longer purify themselves):

> The lesson of the whole matter is as simple and plain as it is persistently denied by a romantic pioneer vanity; and our true pride, as we look back to those days of sturdy and sinful life, must be, not that the pioneers could so successfully show by their popular justice their undoubted instinctive skill in self-government—although indeed, despite all their sins, they showed such a skill also; but that the moral elasticity of our people is so great, their social vitality so marvelous, that a community of Americans could sin as fearfully as, in the early years, the mining community did sin, and could yet live to purify itself within so short a time, not by a revolution, but by a simple progress from social foolishness to social steadfastness. Even thus a great river, for an hour defiled by some corrupting disturbance, purifies itself, merely through its own flow, over its sandy bed, beneath the wide and sunny heavens. [33]

Now the history of Royce's California is the history of relocated Americans, pulled by the land and the chance of a fresh start. Whatever the persuasion (and the spectrum embraced a wide number of social, political, and religious convictions), the assumption operative was an acceptance of the dramatic enhancement of one's possibilities by the presence of uncommitted land and a variety of nature experiences. Such an assumption was operative earlier in the century on the Eastern frontier, as witnessed by a text on the comparatively simple move from Old Virginia to Western Virginia. What greater testament to the moral and political liberation which results from the experience of nature, than at the Virginia Convention of 1830, when a Western Virginia delegate was heard to say:

> But sir, it is not the increase of population in the West which this gentleman ought to fear. It is the energy which the mountain breeze and western habits import to these emigrants. They are regenerated, politically I mean, sir. They soon become *working politicians*; and the difference, sir, between a *talking* and a *working* politician is immense. The Old Dominion has long been celebrated for producing great orators; the ablest metaphysicians in policy; men that can split hairs in all abstruse questions of

political economy. But at home, or when they return from Congress, they have negroes to fan them asleep. But a Pennsylvania, a New York, an Ohio or a western Virginia statesman, though far inferior in logic, metaphysics, and rhetoric to an old Virginia statesman, has this advantage, that when he returns home he takes off his coat and takes hold of the plow. This gives him bone and muscle, sir, and preserves his republican principles pure and uncontaminated.[34]

The theme of "regeneration," spurred on by land, uttered here in a traditional political setting, reached its zenith of intensity in the hundreds of nineteenth-century American experimental communities. What had been European visions, festering with frustration, found their way into American life as communities capable of covenanting on available land, often free. These communities, most often extremely critical of American society, had the possibility of working out a range of beliefs relative to free love, socialism, or the mysteries of diet. The availability of land enabled a fair test [35] to be made of the claims for viability of these life styles. Furthermore, the ensuing relevance of certain aspects of their vision was made possible by the stretch of time, in some cases several generations, during which they could maintain the original character of their communities.

Given the opportunities of land and the extensive time in which to operate, the failure of a new community, experimental or otherwise, was not a crushing blow. Failure was not due to repression or the absence of opportunity but rather to the inadequacy of the idea and its implementation before the test of time. Even as late as the depression of the thirties in our century, Americans were not prone to the experience of alienation and cynicism, now so deeply rooted in American life. [36] But the erosion of belief in endless options, generated by nature, and in the passing of time as liberating has now become a major touchstone of contemporary American society. This development is not unrelated to the fantastic growth of the American city and the begrudged emergence of urban man.

In a word, we have lost our access to experimental space. This is true not only of the great cities, where the vast majority of us now live, but of Butte, Montana or Burlington, Iowa or Zuñi Pueblo, New Mexico, where the disenfranchised huddle together under the ironically cruel aegis of an extraordinary yet private natural setting managed by absentee ownership. The revisionist historians notwithstanding, Frederick Jackson Turner was correct; the closing of the frontier, however symbolic rather than statistical it may have been at the turn of the century, was to spell the inevitable end of a deeply ingrained style. The deeper problem is whether the loss of experimental space will spell also the loss of the experimental temper in America. To put it idiomatically, can rehabilitation replace relocation as the locus for prophetic vision and even more broadly based experimental communities? Or must we accede to those culture prophets, powerful and incisive in their own way, like N. O. Brown, for whom the city is already an Armageddon from which we must take nomadic flight, or Charles Reich, who offers us a quasi-revolutionary re-Greening of America.

The new rhetoric is often fed from two sources, nature nostalgia and a longstanding corollary, the conviction that the city is a trap. So long as our image of the city is a function of our image of nature, we shall intensify our hostility to urban life and our negative judgment will be self-fulfilling. As the actuality of nature recedes in our life, our nostalgia for it becomes increasingly riddled with unreality and innocence about its complexity and dangers. Only a radically reconstituted image of the city will provide us with a new resource for structuring once again a sense of option and experiment as continuous with everyday life. Let us sketch some of the obstacles to such a reconstitution.

THE CITY AS CONTEXT

> And the critical rhythm of a city is the sequence of closing hours, the city's play with the order of the eternal sun.
>
> —Robert Kelly

I isolate several characteristics of our image of the city, which, by no means exhaustive, are nonetheless revealing. Even a brief analysis of these characteristics will provide us with a different perspective from which to view both the plight of urban man and some of the directions necessary for the amelioration of his future.

The first characteristic is double-pronged, with the interacting resonance of a tuning fork. On the one hand, we lament the city as being without nature. On the other hand, the nature we have in mind in such a lamentation and about which we are nostalgic, is stripped of its most forbidding qualities; loneliness, unpredictability, and the terrors of the uninhabitable. Witness the innocence in this comment from Dallas Lore Sharp, a turn of the century commuter from a suburb just outside of Boston.

> And this our life, exempt from public haunts and those swift currents that carry the city-dweller resistlessly into the movie show, leaves us caught in the quiet eddy of little unimportant things—digging among the rutabagas, playing the hose at night. [37]

For the most part, the nature envisioned by urban and suburban man is one that has been domesticated by the very qualities of the city which we take to be unnatural. Commenting on an earlier form of nature nostalgia, Lewis Mumford points to the too often overlooked grubbiness of the open road. He writes in *The Golden Day:*

> The vast gap between the hope of the Romantic Movement and the reality of the pioneer period is one of the sardonic jests of history. On one side the bucolic innocence of the Eighteenth Century, its belief in a fresh start, and its attempt to achieve a new culture. And over against it, the epic march of the covered wagon, leaving behind it deserted villages, bleak cities, depleted soils, and the sick and exhausted souls that engraved their epitaphs in Mr. Masters' Spoon River Anthology. [38]

And recall Van Wyck Brook's description of the America of Emerson's time. "Alas for America! An air loaded with poppy and all running to leaves, to suckers, to tendrils, to miscellany, dispersion and sloth. A wilderness of capabilities, of a many-turning Ulyssean culture; an irresistibility like Nature's, and, like Nature, without conscience." [39]

I make no attempt here to deprecate the majesty of nature nor, as I tried to make clear above, to deny its real capacity as a setting for distinctive social and political growth. Under the press of nostalgia, however, we strip both nature and city of ambivalence, in a bizarre reversal of the wilderness and paradise theme. We now name the city a jungle and ascribe habitability in proportion to our distance away from it. Indeed, we often seem to give the city credence only to the extent that we are able to import nature, to "green" it. Vest-pocket parks and isolated city trees receive our affection while we allow public conveyances, building facades, and other urban artifacts to deteriorate. We seem oblivious to the fact that efforts at "greening" such as Golden Gate Park in San Francisco are often masterpieces of artifact and directly attributable to urban man's management of nature.

As a matter of fact, in our time artifacts shape the entire context of nature. Our American culture has long succumbed to the principle of accessibility on demand, and as heightened by modern technology, particularly the automobile and the airplane, has successfully driven out nature in the sense of "wilderness," which, *a fortiori*, denies accessibility. We resist facing up to the loss of wilderness in America. In the more than two hundred photographs accompanying Freeman Tilden's aforementioned book on *The National Parks*, hardly an automobile is to be seen, but for those of us who have visited those parks and natural monuments, automobiles are omnipresent along with the roads, souvenir stands, and the apparently self-propagating beer can. [40] Turning a wilderness into a park is, after all, a gentle form of urbanization.

Our innocence about the artifactuality of our experience of nature interacts with our failure to form any better image of the city. On one side, we harbor a deep conviction (perhaps prejudice is a better word) of the superiority of the organic over the inorganic, of the natural over the artifactual. Non-organic material becomes at best functional and at worst dehumanizing, saved only by the arbiters of the aesthetics of high culture as it is present in acceptable architecture, museums, and outdoor sculpture. The latter become for many critics of the city the only redeeming features of urban life. Peter L. Marks, for example, in an essay on "A Vision of Environment," tells us that New York is "far too large" but that one should have a city the size of Minneapolis so as to preserve the "urban amenities," which he lists as "museums, galleries, theaters, opera, etc." [41] Such amenities are sought by a very small percentage of city people and they in no way represent the marvels of urban design, the intensity of urban interaction, or the complexity of urban possibility. Many critics of the city have no sense of the pulse of city life except that prescribed by those cultural canons continuous with the lives of the critics. [42] Given such an interpretive context, as we move through the alleged travail of everyday experience, we seem reduced to the impropriety and therefore the social inability to generate non-organic aesthetic metaphors able to provide the security and affection nostalgically traceable to nature metaphors. [43]

The contrasts between "Naturals" and urban materials are inevitably invidious. Grass is soft whereas wood and metal are hard. The sense of touch has either eroded, as with regard to cloth and wood, or never developed as with regard to aluminum, plastics, and the vast range of synthetics. Woodland light is diaphanous and playful, but city light as refracted from giant slabs of glass is arching and brittle. Dung is earthy and a sign of life, whereas axle-grease is dirty and a necessary burden. Many of us were taught as children to distinguish between the clean dirt of nature and the dirty dirt of the playground and the street. Why is it that "swinging on birches" is affectionate and wistful but sitting on curbs is pouty and "hanging out"? Such contrasts are endless, and they are maddening because they distort and repress one entire side of our experience—or, more accurately, if we are honest with ourselves, for most of us our *only* direct experience.

The source of this prejudice is only partially nature nostalgia and the historical seduction of its metaphors. From another vantage point, a more decisive characteristic emerges, namely, that we have failed to articulate our distinctively city experience in aesthetic terms. Just as for decades we have taught multi-racial, multi-ethnic children in the context of a bland, WASPish world, so too have we taught children in a vague combination of a gentle nature-setting and appeals to the values of high culture. Such a pedagogy continues to be oblivious to the teeming relational fabric of urban experience and to the rich nutrients of technological style which children would soak up, as if to the manner born, if so encouraged. Unfortunately, we have held fast to the style and language of traditional pedagogy and, as such, have missed the startling idiomatic evolution from nature language to industrial language, to say nothing of the recent emergence of electronic language.

Urban alienation proceeds from the bifurcation of lived experience and institutional formulation, particularly on the part of the schools, churches, and social-political agencies. The truth is that for hordes of urban children, the argot of street language provides their fundamental education, their coming to consciousness. Unsanctioned as experiences, these sensibilities and insights ride beneath the surface of personal life, unable to bring the person into an acceptable creative life. Our task is to sanction and celebrate these processes of urban living, within the confines of urban institutions. Speaking only of the schools, we must learn, for example, how to integrate the powerful message of jazz, with its emphasis on improvisation, processive unity, and indirect communication (each an urban style). We must learn of the vast array of city materials and generate novel non-nature metaphors to describe our ways of experiencing them. We must learn how to personalize our evaluations of ordinary experiences to render them aesthetic, commensurate with new materials, new techniques, and new anticipations. Could not our watchword be the penetrating remark of John Dewey: "Even a crude experience, if authentically an experience, is more fit to give a clue to the intrinsic nature of esthetic experience than is an object already set apart from any other mode of experience"[44]? These strategies will aid in overcoming one of the deepest and most pervasive sources of our alienation, the separation of the affective life from the processes of urban experience. As strategies they assume, however, a turning back of still another characteristic of our image of the city, that is, our sense of space.

City space is enclosed space, and therein we find a crisis for urban man. As we have attempted to show above, the primary meaning of nature for America was the presence of open space, with its corollary, a sense of time as prospective and fruitful. In the last twenty years, as the diagnosis of the city has become increasingly negative, we have made attempts to restructure it. Subtly but powerfully under the rubric of urban reclamation and renewal we have re-embodied this hankering for open space. We failed to realize that people brought to consciousness in enclosed space had interiorized their sense of time and endowed the immediate environment with the drama of landmarks, whether they be funeral parlors, candy stores, playgrounds, or street processes. Largely unarticulated, this sense of time was a way of protecting the city-dweller from the rapid but pyramidal pace. Experience in the city was hectic, intensive, and escalatory, but not spatially expensive. Entire lives, even generations, were lived out on a single street, known affectionately as the "block."[45] In such an environment it was necessary to structure "stabiles," moments of security and repetition, as a base from which to participate in activities which far outstripped the natural sense of pace and which multiplied novelties at a rate quite beyond personal absorption, let alone comprehension.

Many years ago, the building of the then great apartments on Riverside Drive in New York City occasioned Henry James' comment that they were merely holding the spot for whatever was to replace it.[46] As the pace quickened, each city-dweller structured his or her own version of the environment, developing in either personal terms or in closely-knit communal terms what Kevin Lynch has called nodal points, ways of comfortably and knowingly experiencing the environment. Nodes are points, "the strategic spots in a city into which an observer can enter and which are the intensive foci to and from which he is traveling." [47] These nodal points, not to be confused with landmarks, are too often assumed to be large and obvious, as squares, powerful buildings, or boulevards; more often they are intensive refinements of one's movement thru city-space, the feel of a small street, a lobby, a stoop, a bar, a subway stop, refined even to the north or south entrance. In effect, they are embodiments of intimacy, urban style. They are ways of domesticating the rush of city life. They are sources of affection. Listen to a young black student at Queens College conclude his poem of praise to Harlem.

> 'Cause we own the night
> And the streets and the sounds and the air itself
> And the life is there
> And the movement is there
> And all of our energy
> And the spirit is there
> On through the night
> And right through the dawn
> Through those wide/funky/
> Bad/
>   Black/
>   Streets [48]

Any attempt at massive urban transformation which fails to take into account the deep feeling that people have for their environment, however objectively inadequate, is doomed to failure. The difficulty with extensive relocation is not simply the wait to enter a new home, although that wait is often cruel and abortive. Nor is it simply the loss of an apartment or dwelling. It is the destruction of those nodal points which not only took generations to web into the seam of personal experience but acted as a subtle resource for coping with the massive energy of the city at large. [49] Home, then, is not simply the apartment or even the building. Rather it is correlative with a wider range of experience, including neighborhood and city-region or just accessibility to the familiar. In his profound essay "Grieving for a lost Home," Marc Fried [50] evokes the sadness of those residents who were bullied out of their homes in the West End of Boston. Although many interpersonal relations could be kept in the new location, it was the loss of spatial identity for which they grieved. What is striking about Fried's findings is the extensive presence of bodily responses to the loss. Many persons reported serious depression, nausea, and weeping. Deep in our psyche we are profoundly attached to the allegedly lifeless forms of the urban scene, our streets, lights, and sounds.

The need would seem to be to learn the techniques of rehabilitation rather than fall prey to the precipitous use of the scissoring of spatial relocation. We have some small signs of an increased sensitivity to this need. In New York City, fifty-nine residents of a neighborhood called Corona, led by the urban rhetoric of Jimmy Breslin, staved off relocation and are now struggling to maintain their community against the power of official policy. Even minor relocation was thought to be painful and excessive, for as Francis X. Clines wrote in *The New York Times*, the relationships were, after all, "structural as well as human."

> The job of relocating houses could prove as delicate as heart surgery, for there is an attractive crazy-quilt of structural and human relationships present. For example, Mrs. Thomas Manfre has a house, marked by a lawn madonna, that looks to the rear unto her husband's boyhood home, where a niece now lives. Her 70 year old mother lives off to the side in a separate home, small and brown with a pigeon coop on the roof.
>
> All three are as one in her family's diary, Mrs. Manfre explained. "There have been deaths here and my brother Joey was born here," she said. [51]

We are under obligation to develop an enriched understanding of the relationship between urban structure and urban person. We must develop insight into the time of city-space and the space of city-time. And we must search for a way to render our bodies as continuous with technological artifact as they were with the environs of nature. We have to celebrate this continuity and build accordingly.

If we fail in these tasks, contemporary urban man will simply be in place and as such detached from the processes of living. But, as Royce [52] warns us, the detached individual without deep feeling for his environment dilutes the energies necessary to build communities. And when under duress, the detached individual abandons restraint and, out of disrespect for the variety of life styles, moves to suppress them. We should be warned that nature nostalgia detaches us from the urban present and promulgates condescension, disinterest, and eventually hostility. For better or worse, American man is now urban man, or at the least, megapolitan man. Nature nostalgia, no matter how subtle, does not serve him well. It is time for a turning and a celebrating of the dazzling experiences we have but do not witness for all to share. The city is now our home; in the most traditional and profound sense of the word, it is our land.

NOTES

1. A cardinal example of generalizations creating their own evidence is to be found in David Riesman, Nathan Glazer and Reuel Denney, *The Lonely Crowd* (New Haven, 1950). Our deep contemporary self-consciousness about directedness and manipulation dates from that book.
2. Cf. Daniel Boorstin, *The Image: A Guide to Pseudo-Events in America* (New York, 1964).
3. Cf. Leo Marx, "Pastoral Ideals and City Troubles," *The Fitness of Man's Environment* (Washington, 1968), pp. 142-143. Marx claims that the contention of an anti-urban bias as existent in American literature is a misreading of the metaphoric intention of that tradition. He may be correct about the "intention" but the fact is that the popular interpretation of American literature has sustained a nature romanticism and a distrust of the city.
4. Cf. George H. Williams, "The Enclosed Garden in the Wilderness of the New World," *Wilderness and Paradise* (New York, 1962), pp. 98-131. cf. also Roderick Nash, *Wilderness and the American Mind* (New Haven, 1967).
5. Cf. Edward L. Morgan, *Visible Saints* (Ithaca, N.Y., 1962), pp. 67-73, and Daniel B. Shea Jr. *Spiritual Autobiography in Early America* (Princeton, 1968).
6. For a brilliant analysis of the edenic theme in America, cf. Charles L. Sanford, *The Quest for Paradise: Europe and the American Moral Imagination* (Urbana, Ill. 1961).
7. Morton and Lucia White, *The Intellectual Versus the City* (New York, 1962), p. 19.
8. Samuel Sewall, "Phaenomena," in Perry Miller and Thomas H. Johnson, *The Puritans* (New York, 1963), I, 377.
9. Jonathan Edwards, "Personal Narrative," in Clarence H. Faust and Thomas H. Johnson (eds), *Jonathan Edwards* (New York, Wang, 1962), p. 67.
10. Cited in Perry Miller, "Nature and the National Ego," *Errand into the Wilderness* (New York, 1956), p. 210.
11. Miller, art. cit., p. 211.
12. Cited in Williams, op. cit., p. 130.
13. Cited in Freeman Tilden, *The National Parks* (New York, 1970), p. 22.
14. Thomas Jefferson, *Notes on the State of Virginia* (New York, 1964), query 414, pp. 157-158.
15. Jefferson, op. cit., p. 158.
16. Cf. Morton and Lucia White, op. cit., for an excellent survey of the deep-seated animus against the city that pervades American thought. The Whites, however, seriously underplay the spiritual significance of the land in American life.

17. John M. Anderson, *The Individual and the New World* (State College, Pa., Bald Eagle Press, 1955), p. 12.
18. Lucy Lockwood Hazard, *The Frontier in American Literature* (New York, 1927), p. 152.
19. Ralph Waldo Emerson, "The American Scholar," *The Complete Works of Ralph Waldo Emerson* (Boston, 1904), I, 95.
20. Leo Marx, *The Machine in the Garden: Technology and the Pastoral Idea in America* (New York, 1967), p. 232.
21. Emerson, "Culture," *Works*, VI, 153.
22. Ibid.
23. Carl Bode (ed.), *Collected Poems of Henry Thoreau* (Baltimore, 1964), p. 135.
24. Perry Miller, *Nature's Nation* (Cambridge, 1967).
25. Anderson, op. cit., p. 41.
26. Sidney E. Mead, *The Lively Experiment* (New York, 1963), p. 5.
27. Cf. Leslie Fiedler, *The Return of the Vanishing American* (New York, 1969), p. 187, for a similar remark.
28. Cf. The excellent chapter on "The Mountain Man" in Henry Nash Smith, *Virgin Land: The American West as Symbol and Myth* (New York, 1957), p. 88-98.
29. Emerson, Introduction to "Nature" *Works*, I. 3.
30. Cited in Smith, op. cit., p. 296, n. 4.
31. William James, *The Meaning of Truth* (New York, 1909), p. 111.
32. This passage, with slight changes, is taken from an earlier effort to ground an American metaphysics of history. Cf. John J. McDermott, *The American Angle of Vision* (West Nyack, Cross Currents Paperback, 1966).
33. Josiah Royce, *Basic Writings of Josiah Royce*, ed. John J. McDermott (Chicago, 1969), I, 117. Cf. also the chapter on "The Temper of the West" by James Bryce in *The American Commonwealth* (London, 1891), II, 696-706, for a vivid description of open land from a European point of view.
34. Cited in Frederick Jackson Turner, "The Significance of the Frontier in American History," *Frontier and Section*, ed. Ray Allen Billington (New York, 1961), p. 57.
35. Out of an extensive literature, I will mention only William Hinds, *American Communities*, first published 1875 (reprinted New York, 1961).
36. Compare contemporary social diagnosis with the reports of the depression as found in *The Great Depression*, ed. David A. Shannon (New York, 1960) and Studs Terkel, *Hard Times* (New York, 1970).
37. Cited in Peter J. Schmitt, *Back to Nature—The Arcadian Myth in Urban America* (New York, 1969) p. 20. For many further instances of such nostalgia cf. Samuel R. Ogden, ed., *America the Vanishing—Rural Life and the Promise of Progress* (Brattleboro, Vt., 1969).
38. Lewis Mumford, *The Golden Day* (Boston, 1957), p. 38.
39. Van Wyck Brooks, "Emerson at Sea," in Carl Bode, ed., *Ralph Waldo Emerson* (New York, 1968), p. 68.
40. By contrast, see the stark reality in instances of urban photography, cf. e.g. the remarkable set of photographs in Susan Cahill and Michele F. Cooper, edd., *The Urban Reader* (New York, 1971).
41. Peter L. Marks, "A Vision of Environment," *The American Scholar*, 40 (Summer, 1971), 426. This essay is a utilization, albeit imaginative, of nature-nostalgia, revealing contempt for city life, which he describes by reference to the cliche, "urban anonymity."

42. What, for example, are we to make of this broadside from the landscape architect Ian McHarg? "I contend that ... the modern city inhibits life, that it inhibits man as an organism, man as a social being, man as a spiritual being, and that it does not even offer adequate minimum conditions for physiological man; that indeed the modern city offers the least humane physical environment known to history" ("Man and Environment," in Leonard J. Duhl, *The Urban Condition* [New York, 1969] p. 49).

43. For a discussion of urban aesthetic metaphors, cf. John J. McDermott, "Deprivation and Celebration: Suggestions for an Aesthetic Ecology," in James Edie, ed., *New Essays in Phenomemology* (Chicago, 1969) pp. 116-130.

44. John Dewey, *Art as Experience* (New York, 1950), p. 11.

45. Even in a terribly afflicted neighborhood, the "block" maintained a deep spiritual hold on its residence. Cf. the extraordinary photographic essay by Herb Goro, *The Block* (New York, 1970).

46. Cited in Ray Ginger, *Modern American Cities* (Chicago, 1969), p. 3.

47. Kevin Lynch, *The Image of the City* (Cambridge, 1959) p. 47. Cf. also the refreshing experimental perspectives in Stanley Milgram, "The Experience of Living in Cities," *Science*, 167 (March 13, 1970), 1461-1468. Some of these perspectives are taken into consideration in the exciting new work of Paolo Soleri. Cf. Donald Wall, *Visionary-Cities: The Archology of Paolo Soleri* (New York, 1971).

48. Richie Orange, "Harlem," in Cahill and Cooper, op. cit., p. 143.

49. For a poignant description by young Juan Gonzales of "his being renewed" into a project, cf. Charlotte Leon Mayerson, "Two Blocks Apart," in Cahill and Cooper, op cit., pp. 76-81. Cf. also the review article by Roger Sale, "Cities and the City," *New York Review of Books*, January 28, 1971, p. 40, where he tells of the ramifications in the taking down of a basketball hoop on a city block.

50. Cf. Marc Fried, "Grieving for a Lost Home," in Duhl, op. cit., pp. 151-171.

51. Francis X. Clines in *The New York Times*, December 2, 1970, p. 43.

52. Cf. Josiah Royce, "The Hope of the Great Community," in *Basic Writings*, p. 1156.

THE FAMILY AS UTOPIAN RETREAT FROM THE CITY:

The Nineteenth-Century Contribution

KIRK JEFFREY

Can society ever be constituted upon principles of universal Christian brotherhood? The believing Christian, the enlightened philosopher, answer—IT CAN. Will this organization commence with the entire race of man? with existing governments? or with small isolated communities? Doubtless, the principles of this new organization must be matured in the hearts and lives of individuals, before they can be embodied in any community, but when the new organization commences, it will doubtless be in small communities.[1]

The foundation of our free institutions is in our love, as a people, for our homes. The strength of our country is found, not in the declaration that all men are free and equal, but in the quiet influence of the fireside, the bonds which unite together the family circle. The corner-stone of our republic is the hearth-stone. . . . From the corroding cares of business, from the hard toil and frequent disappointments of the day, men retreat to the bosom of their families, and there, in the midst of that sweet society of wife and children and friends, receive a rich reward for their industry, and are reminded that their best interests are inseparable from public and social morality. . . . The feeling that here, in one little spot, his best enjoyments are concentrated . . . gives a wholesome tendency to [a man's] thoughts, and is like the healing oil poured upon the wounds and bruises of the spirit.[2]

DURING THE YEARS from about 1800 to 1870, and particularly after 1825, the values and expectations about family life which many Americans share today became implanted in middle-class American culture for the first time. These included beliefs

An assistant professor of history at Carleton College, Mr. Jeffrey is working on a study of the family in Jacksonian America and on a biography of William A. Alcott, a nineteenth-century sexual adviser and dietary reformer.

about the nature and proper behavior of women and children, attitudes about sex which were widely accepted well into the twentieth century, and a general sense of sharp disjunction between the private world of the family and the larger society. This last assumption pervaded the writings of the popular moralists and advisers of that age—the physicians, phrenologists, clergymen, "scribbling women," and others who instructed middle-class Americans about their "duties and conduct in life." In the sermons and novels, the magazines and hortatory literature of the mid-nineteenth century, they asserted over and over that home was a distinct sphere, an enclave emphatically set apart from the activities and priorities of "the world," as they usually called the non-domestic part of their society. Associated with this idea was a second one which could be stated in a good many ways but which amounted to an affirmation that, ultimately, the individual found meaning and satisfaction in his life at home and nowhere else.

Our ancestors thus were encouraged to nurse extravagant hopes for the domestic realm. Whether they regarded home as an utter and permanent retreat from life in a shocking and incomprehensible social order, or as a nursery and school for preparing regenerate individuals who would go forth to remake American society, they agreed that domestic life ought to be perfect and could be made so. Through careful design of the home as a physical entity, and equally painstaking attention to the human relationships which would develop within it, the family could actually become a heaven on earth. Many of the significant features and patterns of middle-class family life in the nineteenth century, as well as significant points of strain, tension, and guilt, arose directly from these extravagent expectations.

A risky but potentially illuminating way of coming to terms with dominant American ideas about the family both in that day and in our own may be to analyze the middle-class family as a kind of utopian community, analagous in many respects to the more famous communities which some reformers attempted to plant and nurture during those same decades prior to the Civil War, when recognizably modern family patterns were developing in some parts of American society. Certainly three utopian themes—retreat, conscious design, and perfectionism—pervaded nineteenth-century writings about the family.[3]

What strikes one immediately, as one reads into the ephemeral popular literature of that era, is the intense seriousness with which middle-class writers discussed the home and the family. Often their words seem comical as they strain for the sonorous phrase, the classical allusion, which may succeed in capturing that intensity, that seriousness. "Home!—sweet word and musical!" wrote Mrs. Lydia Sigourney, a noted household poet, "key-tone of the heart, at whose melody, as by the harp of Orpheus, all the trees in its garden are moved, holy word! refuge from sadness and despair, best type of that eternal rest, for which we look, when the journey of life is ended!"[4] This gush was typical of many writers in a sentimental and declamatory age; beneath it, though, was a serious statement. Others could be equally effusive, equally serious: "Home! the very word calls up a thousand feelings of thrilling interest; what ear is there so dull as not to hear it with delight? what heart so cold as not to respond with pleasure to the welcome sound?"[5] Still another writer asked, "Is there any brain so dull into which [the word 'home'] does not flash with a gush of suggestive congruous fascinations?"[6]

In Mrs. Sigourney's statement the dominant theme is retreat. In this connection it is noteworthy that idealized homes of the nineteenth century were invariably described in the context of a generalized, usually sentimentalized rural setting, surrounded by gardens and orchards. An entirely typical description is the following, from Mrs. A. J. Graves's novel *Girlhood and Womanhood* (1844). Here one of the heroines gazes for the first time at the landscape around her family's new home:

> A beautiful prospect stretched away before her. A fine range of green, softly swelling hills, bounded the horizon, behind which the sun was setting, in all the splendor of a richly tinted canopy of clouds. At their base, a lovely valley lay in shadow, through which a stream was gliding, fringed here and there with clumps of trees and shrubs, and upon its grassy banks, her father's herds were quietly grazing. A fine grove of old oaks rose beneath the window, whose trunks were lighted up with the red rays of the declining sun, and the green sward from which they sprung, was beautifully varied by long lines of sunshine and lengthened shadows, as intervening trees or intermediate spaces admitted, or obscured the brilliant hues of sunset.[7]

The language of this description, clotted with "softly swelling hills," "grassy banks," and "green sward," suggests that such scenes—which can be found quite frequently in popular fiction and illustrations—were debased pastorals: middle-class Americans, that is, regarded the most important feature of the ideal home as its location in ordered natural surroundings. But so great was the gulf between aspiration and the social realities of the nineteenth century, and so unequipped were most writers for the task of discovering adequate ways of relating the two, that they fell back upon stale literary conventions.

The hortatory writings of the same period also betrayed the same assumptions. In their massive and famous compendium of domestic advice entitled *The American Woman's Home*, Catharine Beecher and her sister Harriet Beecher Stowe made the rural home their ideal model despite the fact that their audience was largely urban. Much of their instruction on matters domestic, the sisters explained, "is chiefly applicable to the wants and habits of those living either in the country or in such suburban vicinities as give space of ground for healthful outdoor occupation in family

"The Christian Home," from Catharine Beecher and Harriet Beecher Stowe, *The American Woman's Home: or Principles of Domestic Science* (New York, 1869).

service. . . ." They offered advice on the cultivation of flowers, fruits, and vegetables, and the care of "horse, cow, and dairy." "Each and all of the family, some part of the day," they asserted, should "take exercise in the pure air, under the magnetic and healthful rays of the sun. Every head of a family should seek a soil and climate which will afford such opportunities. Railroads, enabling men toiling in cities to rear families in the country, are on this account a special blessing."[8]

This was in 1869. As the illustration of "The Christian Home" and phrases such as the one about "magnetic and healthful rays" suggest, the Beecher sisters too fell back upon a prettified image of country life which was probably far removed from the mundane realities confronting the average farm family. Home, they were suggesting, belonged neither in the city nor too far away from it on the American frontier. Like Mrs. Graves, they believed that it ought ideally to be found in an ordered but natural setting—that is, a timeless one.

The development of this middle-class cult of the rural home must be understood as a response to the historical experience which members of this group were undergoing during the middle decades of the nineteenth century. What it betrayed was an intense fear, a shock of non-recognition, with which such Americans greeted their society. As Marvin Meyers has remarked of them, they "were not inwardly prepared for the grinding uncertainties, the shocking changes, the complexity and in-direction" of the economic and social order which was beginning to confront them by the 1830's and 1840's.[9] The trends toward rapid change, extreme diversity, and new psychic demands had developed most fully in the larger cities of the Republic by then, and we should recall that the forty years prior to 1860 witnessed a higher rate of urban growth in proportion to total population growth, for the Eastern part of the nation, than at any later time in the century. Hence it was appropriate that the city appear to popular moralists and their readers as a symbol of all that distressed them in society outside the home. The cities housed the slums and immigrants, the gambling-dens and saloons which the Protestant clergy so frequently attacked.

The shocking features of urban life were magnified for many middle-class Americans because they were themselves rural-bred migrants to the city. Their very notable propensity to idealize the villages and farms of their childhood years and to excoriate the cities of their adulthood ones is a good index to the "profound alteration in human experience" which they were undergoing. [10] The present discussion can do no more than offer a few examples from the considerable literature of wailing and gnashing of teeth about the city which was appearing as early as the 1830's. One typical volume by the Reverend John Todd, entitled *The Moral Influence, Dangers and Duties, Connected with Great Cities*, offered readers a comprehensive analysis of urban life. Most striking, according to Todd, was the set of purposes that men pursued in the city: "Wealth and Fashion are the deities which preside over the great city.... [There] you see the young, the ardent, the keen, and the gifted, rushing into these great marts of nations, to court the smiles of Mammon;—all hoping for his gifts." The frenzy and cultural diversity of the city thus alarmed him most. "On all sides ... are the songs and the invitations of pleasure, the snares and the pitfalls covered with flowers.... To these very many yield.... All hope by-and-by to be able to retire on a competency. A few can do it; but what an amazing proportion fall in the race! and the tide rolls on, and they and their hopes are forgotten!" [11]

Here, then, was one central meaning of the city: the frantic and relentless pursuit of wealth, a quest at which few would succeed. It was *the universal unconquerable desire for money*," according to Todd, which both gave the city its *raison d'etre* and rendered it utterly iniquitous. The pursuit of riches was intrinsically evil; but it had some side consequences which further compounded the dangers of urban life, even for those few who might withstand its central mania for riches. Of particular importance among these was the transiency of human ties: "Your acquaintances come and go,—are here to-day, and off to-morrow, and you have hardly time, or opportunity, to form deep attachments. The unceasing hurry, and perpetual pressure for time, prevent our forming those deep attachments which we do in country life." [12]

Similar lessons were purveyed to Americans through the didactic fiction of the same era. In the Reverend Daniel Wise's *Young Man's Counsellor*, for instance, one finds the parable of Arthur—"Arthur in Babylon," as R. Richard Wohl calls it in his delightful evisceration of this cautionary tale. Arthur is a kind of failed Horatio Alger hero; everything he does turns out wrong. Aged nineteen, "educated, handsome, of fascinating manners, and manly spirit," Arthur arrives in "a certain city" determined to make his fortune. Here is the very archetype of the middle-class migrant. But the city, it transpires, contains perils that Arthur is wholly unprepared to withstand. The youth "unhappily fell into dissolute society, and began to run the giddy rounds of deep dissipation." Soon his money is gone and he must pay a bill. Arthur's next error brings down the catastrophe upon him: "he took the fatal step of selling an opera glass, which he had borrowed from a gay friend; and thus paid his bill." Next day Arthur learns to his dismay that friendship in the city is not to be counted upon: "his quondam friend had the heart of a Shylock, and hurried the astonished and mortified young man to the police court."

At this point Arthur collapses: " 'Cut my throat! kill me! trample me to death!' " he howls to his astonished cell-mates. Delirious, he is pronounced by a physician to be "in imminent danger of dying." Bailed out by an anonymous philanthropist, Arthur collapses once again when told that his father has been summoned from the hinterland. " 'I can't see him! I can't—I can't!' " groans the piteous Arthur, and dies just as his "venerable father" enters the room.

Wohl's summary remarks are worth quoting in full:

> This brutal little yarn, so equally devoid of mercy and moderation, was printed as a true story; and was intended, and surely accepted by some, as an edifying and moral tale. Arthur's reckless hysteria, his pathological sense of guilt, his panic, and his egregious moral vanity, are blandly recounted by the author as something just and genteel. The story's excessive melodrama is in itself revealing. The fear and hatred of urban demoralization was so great that its condemnation was correspondingly enormous. The story serves well to polarize city and country, stigmatizing the one and, by implication, unreservedly approving the other. Arthur's downfall commences from the day he comes to the city; in the country he was happy, useful, and ornamental. The city is the villain and Arthur is its victim. [13]

Indictments of the city such as Todd's and Wise's were based on a common nineteenth-century psychological theory: "We all know," wrote Todd, "that familiarity with any thing has a wonderful effect upon our feelings, and that is is a principle in human nature, that what is in itself revolting, will, by familiarity, cease to disgust." [14] By implication, few if any city-dwellers could long hold out against the inevitable taint of experience; sophistication and virtue were incompatible. Indeed, such was precisely the lesson of "Arthur in Babylon."

Thus the necessary conclusion to such a despairing theory of the impact of urban experience was the recommendation that it be avoided entirely. And the only sure way to do so, naturally, was to remain in the country. But there was a second possibility—an outpost of the country, as it were, within city walls. This was, of course, the family; and for those who could not return to rural America, or who found the opportunities of city life too attractive to allow them to heed the warnings of the Todds and the Wises, the second-best choice was to establish a little sphere of peace and order to which they could retreat. Ideally the family ought to be rural; and a later generation, blessed with more efficient means of transportation, would discover that it was possible to commute to the city while still enjoying a home life far removed from its terrors, in houses surrounded by a few hundred square feet of well-trimmed grass. But more than a century ago the essential perception of the city had already been formulated, along with the response which has remained the most popular one for the American middle class: complete retreat.

> We go forth into the world, amidst the scenes of business and of pleasure; we mix with the gay and the thoughtless, we join the busy crowd, and the *heart* is sensible to a desolation of feeling: we behold every principle of justice and of honor, and even the dictates of common honesty disregarded, and the delicacy of our moral sense is wounded; we see the general good, sacrificed to the advancement of personal interest; and we turn from such scenes, with a painful sensation, almost believing that virtue has deserted the abodes of men; again, we look to the *sanctuary* of *home*; there sympathy, honor, virtue, are assembled; there the eye may kindle with intelligence, and receive an answering glance; there disinterested love, is ready to sacrifice every thing at the altar of affection. [15]

For the most part, as such statements indicate, popular writers tended to define the ideal home as an Edenic retreat, a rural haven utterly distinct from the terrors of urban life and the loneliness which could assail men there. As one clergyman put it, home was "a sweet bower of peace and joy in this desert world, where hope brightens, and love gathers its linked, confiding circle;—a blissful retreat for jaded and weary hearts when the busy world drives on its votaries in the train of Mammon and pampered self;—a safe and alluring shelter for *yourselves* amid the vicissitudes of life, becoming more and more the abode of peace and love as the world grows dark without." [16] This conception was nowhere more memorably stated than in Donald Grant Mitchell's bestseller of the 1850's, *Reveries of a Bachelor:*

Sending your blood in passionate flow, is the ecstasy of the conviction that *there* at least you are beloved; that there you are understood; that there your errors will meet ever with gentlest forgiveness; that there your troubles will be smiled away; that there you may unburden your soul fearless of harsh, unsympathizing ears; and that there you may be entirely and joyfully—yourself. [17]

Retreat, companionship, possibly even the surcease from moral striving—these were the elements of Americans' notion of the Edenic home. Sometimes, to be sure, popular writers—often the very same ones—also asserted that home and the surrounding society were vitally connected: that the regenerate family would train up moral children and gradually reform adult males, so that ultimately, through thousands of such trickles of perfected individuals, a mighty tide of social reform would sweep aside all the evil features of nineteenth-century society. Through "family discipline and instruction," rather than any public institutions or agencies, Americans could achieve some deeply-desired goals: "the preservation of manners, the maintenance of religion, and the perpetuity of national freedom." [18] But this second conception of the relationship between family and society, like the first, posited no extended day-to-day contact between the two "spheres." Middle-class Americans, that is, took care to define the social role of the family in such a way that it did not demand many significant forays from home out into the larger society, or even much detailed knowledge of it. Thus both definitions of the ideal home—as perfect retreat or as school for a moral citizenry—were premised upon the assumption that a serious and practically unbridgeable gulf existed between the two spheres, family and society.

In a more extended discussion of the nineteenth-century middle-class family it would be possible to consider the underlying structural changes which certainly stimulated the intense preoccupation in domesticity and the sense of a sharp disjunction. It was not merely the transformation of the outer society but rapid alterations in family patterns themselves which sensitized middle-class Americans to the problem of the family. Notable among these changes, but difficult as yet for the historian to examine with precision, were a disruption of the internal unity of the family due to the separation of the husband's work from the home in nineteenth-century cities, and the attenuation of informal ties to relatives and neighbors which had characterized rural and village life. The latter development was particularly significant, for without a rich web of kinship and friendship, urban middle-class family members were seriously hindered from meeting other city-dwellers on intimate terms, gaining detailed knowledge about the processes of urban life, or becoming more involved in these processes. In fact, one might hazard the guess that the isolation wrought by the withering of kin ties probably contributed as much as the chaos of the urban environment itself to the notable middle-class alienation from the city by mid-century. [19]

The middle-class sense of a gulf between family and society was by no means inevitable and natural, and it had not existed, as far as historians can tell, in colonial America. I have suggested that the growth of this perception can be understood as the *consequence* of social changes, some of them external to the family and others within the family and kinship system itself. Now I want to raise a different question: Did the nineteenth-century sense of a disjunction between the two realms in turn act as a *cause* of other changes in family and society, or at least reinforce changes already occurring?

Let us first consider the results for intimate family life of the cult of the idyllic home. It seems that life in the isolated, Edenic homes of the middle class, to the degree that the perfectionist definition of home was taken seriously, probably exacerbated the compulsive self-examination of many Protestant, middle-class husbands and wives and enormously increased the burdens of anxiety and guilt which they bore. Here was an unexpected and particularly ironic result of the cult, for it encouraged its votaries to expect near-perfect repose and emotional fulfillment in the domestic sphere.

The precise nature of the difficulties differed for husbands and wives. For husbands, there arose what we may call the "commuting problem." If a virtuous sophistication in the city was truly impossible, as writers like Todd and Wise affirmed, how then could men dare to leave home at all to pursue careers in American society? Or if they did leave, even for a few hours a day, what would happen to their wives and families when they returned? This quandry, arising from the literal way in which middle-class Americans took their own definitions of the pure home and the depraved world, was at the center of many novels and stories of the period. In no case were popular authors able to fuse domestic and worldly experience into a coherent whole.

One typically spectacular expression of the problem appeared in a story entitled "The Prodigal's Return," by Timothy Shay Arthur. [20] Arthur, whose temperance novel *Ten Nights in a Bar-Room* rivalled even *Uncle Tom's Cabin* in sales, published over one hundred volumes of didactic fiction between 1840 and 1870. In "The Prodigal's Return" young William Enfield leaves home to go to college. His mother's anxious question as he sets out, " 'You won't forget your mother, William?' " sets the theme for the tale. At college William falls under the influence of evil companions, becomes a card-sharper and a prankster, and is finally expelled. He spends years as a professional gambler—the road from college high-jinks to adult depravity was apparently a broad and easy one—but finally experiences an instantaneous conversion in the form of a dream about home and mother. Resolving to put aside his evil ways, William returns to his childhood home and is forgiven by his parents. There he remains, presumably, forever after. This version of the prodigal son parable failed adequately to solve the dilemma of home's relation to the world. What would William Enfield *do* now that he had returned home? Could he be the kind of vigorous, ambitious, independent man that Americans admired, without venturing outside again? Equally important, was it really so easy to put aside everything he had learned and become since leaving home? And was it really true that all experience was worthy only of being forgotten?

A second and even more interesting pattern in popular fiction also tried to deal with the problem posed for men by the notion of two spheres. In this case we find that worldly men, instead of being saved by home and women, destroy the domestic enclave itself. Lydia Maria Child's story "Home and Politics" provides an example. [21] George Franklin and his wife are at first a happy married couple preoccupied with their domestic life together. But "in an evil hour a disturbing influence crossed their threshold. It came in the form of political *excitement*; that pestilence which is forever racing through our land, seeking whom it may devour; destroying happy homes." George's increasing interest in caucuses and campaigns, growing largely out of desire for office and power, draws him away from home night after night. On election night, 1840, while he is gone, his child falls sick and dies. Then in 1844 he loses all his money by betting on Henry Clay; this time his wife goes mad. "When he visits her, she looks at him with strange eyes, and still clinging to the fond ideal of her life, she repeats mournfully, 'I *want* my home. Why don't George come and take me home?' "

Essentially Mrs. Child was wrestling with the same difficulty: experience in the world inevitably changes a person, but the cult of home demanded that one return absolutely intact. Implicit in both stories, and made fully explicit in the numerous volumes of advice to young men during the mid-nineteenth century, was the exhortation for American men to love domestic life and to model themselves after their wives. This suspicion of men and their worldly doings followed necessarily from the Victorian "cult of true womanhood" which placed middle-class women on pedestals and proclaimed that they were naturally more cultured, affectionate, and pious than their husbands. [22] Only by becoming women in significant respects could American men, it seemed, be considered fit for sustained presence in the home.

In concrete terms, this boiled down to a number of extreme demands which popular moralists quite literally expected men to meet. The first was that they stay home—indeed, this was their fundamental commandment to American men. *"Virtue, purity, spiritual excellence* are the great purposes of our being. And where can you acquire these qualities better than at home?" [23] Such writers regarded ambition for fame or fortune as a base impulse, the moral equivalent of uncontrollable lust for sex or gambling. One clergyman lamented, for example, that in many young men

> you may see in the very outset of life a passion for Gain towering above every thing else; so that ease, even the necessary rest of night, time, talents, and not seldom reputation itself, are sacrificed on the altar of Mammon. He, who feels this burning desire to get rich, cares usually but little for the pleasures of home. He is never, indeed, so uneasy as when seated by his own fireside; for he feels, while conversing with his kindred, that he is making no money. And as for fireside reading, there is to him no interest in that; 'he reads no book but his ledger.' [24]

Once at home, men must consult with their wives and defer to them. As purer beings, women were more trustworthy guides on matters of morals and often, too, with respect to more worldly decisions. "Nothing," wrote the health reformer William A. Alcott, "is better calculated to preserve a young man from the contaminations of low pleasures and pursuits, than frequent intercourse [of the Platonic variety, one judges] with the more refined and virtuous of the other sex." [25]

But how could women be safeguarded from the sexual lust of men? Might not husbands prove so coarse and passionate that the purity of their wives, and hence of the home itself, would be endangered? This was an issue of explicit discussion during the generation before 1860. Whether the passions of men resulted from their innately bestial natures or were vastly heightened by worldly experience, men were always perceived in middle-class writing about the home as extreme threats to the peace and unity of the family. The natural conclusion was that husbands must exercise a continual self-restraint in sexual matters, in order to enable wives to remain pure enough to save them through their mild influence. Clearly there was something circular about this line of thought, for if men successfully practiced sexual continence, was that not a good indication that they already had their base propensities well under control? Which was to come first, the influence of the pure wife or masculine self-restraint? Unaware of this problem with their regimen, domestic advisers went right ahead in affirming that "there is no lust in true marriage, and two rightly mated never run to excess in anything in any of the indulgencies [sic] of their natures." [26] In more explicit terms, physicians and others were not shy about spelling out precisely what this meant. Alcott, an extremely popular arbiter on matters of medicine and health, urged late marriage, told young married couples to live with their parents during the early months of marriage, and warned them to refrain from sexual relations during pregnancy and lactation. The rest of the time "one indulgence to each lunar month, is all that the best health of the parties can possibly require." [27]

In the case of middle-class husbands, then, we might say that the demands upon them—that they stay home, practice a continual sexual continence, and model themselves upon their wives—were heavy and almost impossible to carry out to perfection. Yet popular moralists demanded perfection. Moreover, their advice disguised a significant contradiction, for the intimacy and affection which they promised American husbands and wives was probably difficult to achieve in the context of the rigid sexual formality and self-control which the same writers also urged.

For American wives the difficulties arising from the definition of home as a separate and perfect realm were, if anything, more poignant, for women had few alternatives to their domestic role.

Curiously, though, the precise nature of these difficulties has been little noted and discussed by social historians.

While it is an overstatement to speak of the "oppression" or "subjection" of middle-class wives in the nineteenth century, there seems little doubt that they suffered a notable decline in autonomy and morale during the three-quarters of a century following the founding of the American republic. Essentially this decline occurred as an indirect result of underlying changes in family patterns, and particularly in expectations about family life, which we have been examining. Most women in this group failed to perceive the "correct" causes for the sense of desperation which many of them seem frequently to have felt. In particular, they failed to see the unfortunate side-effects of the "cult of true womanhood" which defined them as the pious, pure keepers of the hearthside and bearers of genteel culture.

Almost all middle-class American wives accepted these ideas quite seriously, as far as the historian can tell. They did not regard confinement to the home as an indication that they were oppressed. On the contrary, if home was more pure and joyful, as women were continually assured, then it was a definite privilege to be allowed to remain there, unsullied by the outside world. Over and over again, women writers commented on the exalted position of their sex and thanked men for treating them with the respect which was their due. Thus Mrs. Sarah J. Hale, editor of *Godey's Lady's Book* and probably the most influential spokeswoman for her millions of sisters in nineteenth-century America, dedicated her *Woman's Record* to American men, "who show, in their laws and customs, respecting women, ideas more just and feelings more noble than were ever evinced by men of any other nation." [28]

In the home middle-class wives had an arena in which they exercised much genuine responsibility and power. Their husbands were absent often; yet even when present, men were urged by popular moralists to model themselves after women and treat their wives with affection and deference. But it appears that the very set of ideas which endowned them with significant responsibility and power in the domestic sphere also weighted women with a heavy burden of anxiety and guilt. It was their duty to make home perfect, for only in a perfect home could husbands and children be redeemed and the outside society thereby reformed and saved. Or, to put it another way, only a perfect home could be a genuine alternative, a genuinely Edenic retreat from the horrors of the larger society.

Whether perfection was defined in terms of retreat and affection or training and order, it followed that every mundane household duty of women could be invested with the gravest implications. No matter how apparently routine and trivial, *every last chore* could be made to seem enormously significant. "Who knows but the Mexican war may be traced to an ill-cooked, ill-assorted, contradictory and irritating cabinet dinner?" asked "A Lady of New York" in *The American System of Cookery*. [29] This was an unusually bold claim, or at least an unusually specific one. But many others spoke in the same vein. "It is within your power," Daniel Wise told young American wives, "to create a domestic heaven in the lowliest cottage." [30] Catharine Beecher was especially prominent in the campaign to endow homemakers with a sense of the grave significance of their every action. Her advice books covered dozens of minute topics, abounded with technical illustrations, and always conveyed the message that if such seemingly unimportant matters were not attended to by American wives, the family and society would suffer grievously.

Ideas of this sort obviously led directly to a belief in the pressing need for conscious, sustained domestic training for women. Housekeeping, in fact, was a science "of broad extent, and minute detail. It cannot be grasped without due preparation, any more than a course of history could be achieved without laborious reading." [31] This notion could take ludicrous forms when combined with the ruthless perfectionism of popular moralists. "For my own part," wrote William A. Alcott in *Letters to a Sister; or Woman's Mission*, "I see not how a Christian woman of but common intelligence, should dare . . . to make a loaf of bread without a thorough knowledge of Chemistry." [32] In the same book he summarized the message to American wives: "There is not an act of your lives so small but you should labor with all your might, and resolve, and if necessary re-resolve concerning it." [33]

The task of perfecting the home through ceaseless work and attention to detail was ultimately an impossible one; indeed, the constant effort and bustle of trying to perfect it probably would have ensured that family life would never succeed in being perfectly restful and joyous. But American domestic advisers encouraged women to believe that perfection was really theirs to attain, and that if they failed at it the responsibility was their own and the consequences vast. Inevitably, in a culture which entertained perfectionist dreams and looked to the home for their attainment, women would bear much of the sense of failure and guilt when perfection failed of being achieved.

Perhaps, then, historians should seek indications that middle-class women felt a sense of futility and guilt arising from the inevitable gap between expectations and reality. Presumptive signs of such feelings abound, but as yet little systematic study of this problem has been done. [34] It appears, for one thing, that women devised a number of ways to "drop out" of the domestic role without explicitly rejecting it. One way, of course, was to develop a non-domestic avocation or career in which one continued to pay lip-service to domesticity without personally trying to live up to it. This path was the one taken by many "scribbling women," most of whom apparently felt somewhat uneasy about their effective rejection of domesticity in favor of a literary career, but few of whom were able to face the fact that they had indeed rejected it. [35] A second path was to develop interests in charity work, Sunday School societies, tract societies, sewing circles, or other similar activities which the historian William L. O'Neill has called "social feminism." [36] These pursuits, like journalism and litera-ture, were premised upon two of the fundamental tenets of the "cult of true womanhood": that women were too pure to associate safely with anybody except other women, and that nurture, religion, letters, and the like were peculiarly feminine activities. Still a third avenue was to become involved in movements for political reform, including feminism. Even this alternative to domesticity did not necessarily result in a rejection of prevailing expectations and ideals about women and the home, as O'Neill and others have shown. [37] Another path is less clearly understood from the distance of a century or more, but some women—how many is anybody's guess—dropped out, temporarily or permanently, through sickliness and the use of drugs. By developing vague physical or psychological maladies a woman could reduce to more manageable proportions the expectations focused upon her in her roles as wife, mother, and housekeeper. By turning to patent medicines, many of which were laced with alcohol or narcotic drugs, she could find more immediate and temporary respite. [38]

Let us attempt to summarize the foregoing discussion, and in the process we can perhaps note some consequences for the society at large of the middle-class tendency to perceive a virtually unbridgeable gulf between the domestic and worldly realms.

It seems clear, first, that these nineteenth-century Americans entertained utopian aspirations about the family. At least, they told themselves that the domestic sphere could truly and literally become an isle of bliss in which their hopes for leisure, harmony, and joy could be fulfilled. Even when they affirmed that the family ought to concern itself with moral training of its members, they still emphasized that this would occur through gentle, loving techniques. Thus the ends of family life were emphatically individualistic, libertarian, even anarchic. In the perfected American home that perennial American aspiration, individual freedom, could at last be attained—and without a corresponding increase in social disorder.

In practice, as we have seen, these aspirations were more difficult to realize, even in such a small theater as the family, than most Americans had anticipated. Indeed, it even appears that the aspirations were so high as to breed greater frustration with family life than they might otherwise have been forced to endure. Internally, the perfectionist expectations placed heavy burdens of guilt upon adults of both sexes.

In terms of the relationship between family and community, the middle-class yearning for a small corner of peace in the form of a happy family may actually have furthered the social trends which Americans deplored and which encouraged them to turn inward in the first place: the misgovernment of the city, the frantic race for status through conspicuous consumption, the degradation of politics in the Jacksonian era, and the rest. It is notable in this connection that nineteenth-century writings on the city and on other problems of American society usually betrayed a deep ignorance even as they lamented the national decline and called for reform and renewal. Popular writers and their audience strike one as unable to perceive their society in any complexity; they tended to view it, and particularly the city, in stereotyped images, as a hellish place dotted with brothels, saloons, gambling-dens, race-tracks, and Catholic churches. What brought about this ignorance? The retreat to domesticity was hastened by fear of the city, but also by structural changes such as the withering of ties to kin and neighbors. These probably resulted from the migration of many middle-class families from small towns to cities, and were further exacerbated by the high rates of geographical mobility which apparently prevailed in nineteenth-century cities. [39]

Whatever the cause of the fear of the city and the ignorance about its workings, the point is that middle-class Americans increasingly opted for retreat rather than for active engagement in the life of their society. They thereby ensured that the abuses they perceived would be perpetuated and that their reasons for despairing about their society would grow ever stronger.

The foregoing indictment also raises the question of the "privacy" of the family. Middle-class Americans valued privacy in the nineteenth century as never before. In a sense their isolated families enjoyed a significant amount of it. Certainly this was one of the things implied in the distinction they customarily drew between home and the world. But their privacy was far from complete, and in some ways it has declined further since that time. The family was being penetrated by society at large at the very moment that its members discerned a gulf between family and society. It was being penetrated, most significantly, by the popular novels, magazines, and advice-books of the day. Unthinking, traditional ways of proceeding—in sexual behavior, child nurture, task allocation—were being replaced by impersonal instruction provided by outsiders. Custom was being replaced by fashion.

Thus the vaunted privacy of the middle-class family, its emphatic otherness from the evil world beyond, did not run so deep as many believed. Uprooted, half-educated, self-scrutinizing, middle-class Americans turned eagerly to the new mechanisms which seemed ready to assume responsibility for telling them what to believe and how to behave. The "Jacksonian era," then, may have witnessed not a breakdown of institutions, as some historians contend, but rather the beginnings of a switch in the sources from which Americans would take their cues. [40]

And yet, if total privacy did not really exist, this was due to society's penetration of the family, not to any intense participation of family members in the life of the society. The emerging ideology of the happy family was an outgrowth of the pervasive American ideology called "privatism" by Sam B. Warner, Jr.:

> Already [Warner writes] by the time of the Revolution privatism had become the American tradition. Its essence lay in its concentration upon the individual and the individual's search for wealth. Psychologically, privatism meant that the individual should seek happiness in personal independence and in the search for wealth; socially, privatism meant that the individual should see his first loyalty as his immediate family, and that

a community should be a union of such money-making, accumulating families; politically, privatism meant that the community should keep the peace among individual money-makers, and, if possible, help to create an open and thriving setting where each citizen would have some substantial opportunity to prosper. [41]

One might conclude, then, that middle-class Americans in the mid-nineteenth-century city were able to isolate themselves with sufficient thoroughness to retreat from responsibility for dealing with urban governance and urban reform; but they were unable to isolate themselves to the degree needed for a genuinely different set of values, priorities, and configurations of personal interaction to take hold. Indeed, as one studies the supposedly Edenic family of the urban middle classes, one discovers that the very qualities by which Eden was defined—the possibility for isolation and individual fulfillment—and the implacable perfectionism with which such hopes were pursued, were quintessentially American. To these Americans of the nineteenth century there was no necessary conflict between the demands of domestic life and the desire for personal freedom. Huck Finn may have yearned to light out for the Territory after exposure to domesticity as personified in Miss Watson. But to a great many less adventurous citizens, domesticity itself came to seem a pleasurable and emancipating escape-hatch from the cares and anxieties of life in nineteenth-century society. Or so they thought, at any rate. Huck encountered terrors and dangers in his travels to evade life in society. Perhaps it would have amused and heartened him to be told that his more conventional countrymen also came up against their own obstacles and disappointments in their search for a genuine alternative to urban life in the very midst of the city.

NOTES

1. "Co-operative Associations," *Liberator*, X (December 25, 1840), p. 207; as quoted in Arthur E. Bestor, Jr., *Backwoods Utopias: The Sectarian and Owenite Phases of Communitarian Socialism in America: 1663-1829* (Philadelphia, 1950), p. 19.
2. William G. Eliot, Jr., *Lectures to Young Women* (Boston, 1880 [first published in 1853]), pp. 55-56.
3. The analysis which follows is based on my doctoral dissertation: Family History: The Middle-Class American Family in the Urban Context, 1830-1870 (Department of History, Stanford University, 1972). For further discussion and many more examples the reader is invited to consult that work. I should add that the notion of the family as a utopian community occurred to me only as an afterthought and plays no part in

the dissertation. The dissertation, however, contains discussions of several matters, such as kinship and conjugal role-relationships, which I have largely omitted here.

4. Lydia H. Sigourney, *Whisper to a Bride* (Hartford, 1850), p. 25.
5. "Home," *Ladies' Magazine*, III (May, 1830), p. 217.
6. Timothy Shay Arthur, *Our Homes: Their Cares and Duties, Joys and Sorrows* (Philadelphia, 1856), p. 27.
7. Mrs. A. J. Graves, *Girlhood and Womanhood: or, Sketches of My Schoolmates* (Boston, 1844), pp. 179-80.
8. Catharine Beecher and Harriet Beecher Stowe, *The American Woman's Home: or, Principles of Domestic Science* (New York, 1869), pp. 24-25.
9. Marvin Meyers, *The Jacksonian Persuasion: Politics and Belief* (New York, 1960), p. 11.
10. Michael B. Katz, *The Irony of Early School Reform: Educational Innovation in Mid-Nineteenth Century Massachusetts* (Cambridge, 1968), p. 5.
11. John Todd, *The Moral Influence, Dangers and Duties, Connected with Great Cities* (Northampton, Mass., 1841), pp. 18-20.
12. Ibid., p. 119.
13. Daniel Wise, *The Young Man's Counsellor; or, Sketches and Illustrations of the Duties and Dangers of Young Men*, 4th ed. (Boston, 1851), pp. 196-98; R. Richard Wohl, "The 'Country Boy' Myth and Its Place in American Urban Culture: The Nineteenth-Century Contribution," ed. Moses Rischin, *Perspectives in American History*, III (1969), p. 90.
14. Todd, p. 54.
15. "Home," *Ladies' Magazine*, p. 218.
16. William M. Thayer, *Pastor's Wedding Gift* (Boston, 1854), p. 36.
17. "Ik Marvel," pseud. [Donald Grant Mitchell], *Reveries of a Bachelor; or, A Book of the Heart* (New York, 1893 [first published in 1850]), p. 57.
18. Theodore Dwight, Jr., *The Father's Book; or Suggestions for the Government and Instruction of Young Children, on Principles Appropriate to a Christian Country*, 2nd ed. (Springfield, Mass., 1835), p. 23.
19. Kinship patterns in colonial America are discussed in John Demos, *A Little Commonwealth: Family Life in Plymouth Colony* (New York, 1970) and Philip J. Greven, Jr., *Four Generations: Population, Land, and Family in Seventeenth-Century Andover, Massachusetts* (Ithaca, N.Y., 1970). For a modern sociological discussion of kinship which has implications for the nineteenth century, see Michael Young and Peter Willmott, *Family and Kinship in East London* (Baltimore, 1957).
20. Timothy Shay Arthur, "The Prodigal's Return," in idem, *Stories for Parents* (Philadelphia, 1854), pp. 92-111.
21. Lydia Maria Child, "Home and Politics," *Sartain's Union Magazine of Literature and Art*, III (August, 1848), pp. 43-48.
22. See Barbara Walter, "The Cult of True Womanhood: 1820-1860," *American Quarterly*, XVIII (Summer, 1966), pp. 151-74.
23. Artemus B. Muzzey, *The Young Man's Friend* (Boston, 1836), p. 103.
24. Ibid., p. 102.
25. William A. Alcott, *The Young Man's Guide* (Boston, 1833), p. 247.
26. Charles S. Woodruff, *Legalized Prostitution: or, Marriage as It Is, and Marriage as It Should Be, Philosophically Considered* (Boston, 1862), p. 148.
27. Alcott, *The Physiology of Marriage* (Boston, 1855), passim.

28. Sarah J. Hale, *Woman's Record; or Sketches of All Distinguished Women, from 'the Beginning' till A.D. 1850 (New York, 1853), p. v.*
29. Quoted in *Sartain's Union Magazine of Literature and Art*, I (December, 1847), p. 287.
30. Daniel Wise, *Bridal Greetings: A Marriage Gift* (New York, 1850), p. 84.
31. Lydia H. Sigourney, *Letters to My Pupils* (New York, 1851), p. 115.
32. William A. Alcott, *Letters to a Sister; or Woman's Mission* (Buffalo, 1850), p. 74.
33. Ibid., p. 32.
34. See, however, William R. Taylor and Christopher Lasch, "Two 'Kindred Spirits': Sorority and Family in New England, 1839-1846," *New England Quarterly*, XXXVI (March, 1963), pp. 23-41.
35. See Ann D. Wood, "The 'Scribbling Women' and Fanny Fern: Why Women Wrote," *American Quarterly*, XXIII (Spring, 1971), pp. 3-24. For an interesting older treatment see Gordon S. Haight, *Mrs. Sigourney: The Sweet Singer of Hartford* (New Haven, 1930).
36. William L. O'Neill, *Everyone Was Brave: The Rise and Fall of Feminism in America* (Chicago, 1969), Ch. iii. See also Keith Melder, "Ladies Bountiful: Organized Women's Benevolence in Early 19th-Century America," *New York History*, XLVIII (July, 1967), pp. 231-54.
37. O'Neill, *Everyone Was Brave*; Aileen S. Kraditor, *The Ideas of the Woman Suffrage Movement, 1890-1920* (New York, 1965), esp. Ch. iii.
38. I make this assertion without, as yet, having much evidence about drugs or their connection to the anxieties of women. Some nineteenth-century testimony is to be found in William A. Alcott, *Forty Years in the Wildnerness of Pills and Powders* (Boston, 1859); and Catharine Beecher, *Letters to the People on Health and Happiness* (New York, 1855).
39. The most important recent study of geographical mobility is Stephan Thernstrom and Peter R. Knights, "Men in Motion: Some Data and Speculations about Urban Population Mobility in Nineteenth-Century America," *Journal of Interdisciplinary History*, I (Autumn, 1970), pp. 7-35.
40. This idea was suggested by Professor Daniel H. Calhoun in an unpublished paper entitled "The Authoritarian Character of Jacksonian America," which was read in August, 1968, at the annual meeting of the Pacific Coast Branch of the American Historial Association.
41. Sam B. Warner, Jr., *The Private City: Philadelphia in Three Periods of Its Growth* (Philadelphia, 1968), pp. 3-4.

DAY CARE:

Patchwork, Realization, or Utopia?

PEGGY and PETER STEINFELS

DAY CARE IS an idea whose time has come. That does not necessarily mean it is a good idea, but simply that it is on the national agenda. It is on the national agenda because it is the common interest of a constellation of forces: government bureaucrats concerned with welfare reform, educators concerned with early child development, women concerned with "liberation." Some of these forces see day care as auguring major adjustments in American life, profound changes, for example, in the form of the family or the status of women. Others conceive of day care as a natural addition to present social institutions, an extension of the school system downward, or a substitution for the haphazard babysitting available to working mothers. But serious contemplation of the implications of day care remains strikingly slight, given the massive proportions of the programs many advocates propose.[1] The same person who one moment expresses the belief that "our schools are prisons" may the next moment endorse handing over infants to a large, school-like bureaucracy providing "24-hour day care."

It is, of course, a truism by now that reform measures often finish by defeating the reformers. David Rothman's *The Discovery*

Peggy Steinfels took a degree at New York University, specializing in the history of the family. She has reviewed movies and books for the *National Catholic Reporter* and other journals and is presently writing a book on day care.

Peter Steinfels, Associate for the Humanities at the Institute of Society, Ethics and the Life Sciences, has contributed articles to the *Nation, New York Times Book Review, New American Review, Concilium,* and numerous other publications, as well as to several books.

of the Asylum, which describes the utopian impulses animating the founding fathers of such institutions as asylums, workhouses, orphanages, and prisons, is only the most recent study to give pause to anyone contemplating a major "progressive" social innovation.[2] If one cannot assume that the future of day care lies along these lines, it is partially because some day-care advocates are all too conscious of the dismal past, even if for many of them it only goes back as far as Headstart. Yet such a wide variety of groups and interests is presently pressing for the expansion of day care and child development services, for an equally wide variety of reasons, that it seems inevitable that someone be disappointed. Chicago's Crisis Committee for Day-Care, for example, represents a broad range of organizations from local day-care centers to private welfare agencies to organizations of the three major religious faiths. The National Ad Hoc Coalition on Child Development manages to encompass both the Family Life Division of the U.S. Catholic Conference and Zero Population Growth.

All these groups seem to agree that services to young children and day care in particular need to be expanded. They provide, on both the local and national level, a large, effective, broad-ranging lobbying force promoting legislation, funding, and administrative implementation. Their vigorous lobbying effort grows out of new perceptions about children, families, pre-school education, women, and welfare, set in relation to what some see as a crisis in family life, child-rearing, and education, others see as a necessary adaptation of basic institutions like the family and schools to a rapidly changing technocratic society, and still others as a golden opportunity for introducing new values into American life.

No set of categories devised to characterize this multitude of motivations and hopes can be sewn together without some overlap here or some sawdust leaking at the seams there; nevertheless, duly noting the danger of oversimplification, we would distinguish three attitudes toward the relationship between day care and the general movement of society.

1. Day care as patchwork. This outlook views day-care services essentially as repairing breakdowns in present social institutions. It is a kind of first aid—for fatherless families, for children needing better care and extra educational assistance, for mothers whom economic or emotional difficulties prevent from providing full-time care for their children. Day care helps to compensate for faults in family structure, educational resources, or the economic

system. Goals for day care are thus defined largely by the status quo in "mainstream" society. Day care should bring those disadvantaged in one way or another up to this standard, or keep them from falling below it if hardship strikes the home.

2. Day care as realization. This outlook fundamentally accepts the values and direction of the present society but feels these are far from realized in the status quo. By assuming duties of the home, day care would provide entry into advanced industrial society for a vast number of previously excluded women. Day care would offer to all children an early educational environment employing the best resources the society has developed, thus equipping the greatest possible number of them for successful entry into a rapidly changing society demanding refined skills. Day care would also buttress certain changes in family structure—its loosening, if not is disappearance altogether—already set in motion by the mobility, individualization, and egalitarianism of modern industrialism. Women and children would be freed from the patriarchal, nuclear household. Society would accept new responsibilities for the care and development of children.

3. Day care as utopia. This outlook views day care as a means of renewing society in a way radically discontinuous with the present. The possibility of changing society by infusing new values into the young has always been part of the utopian inheritance. So, too, has been the potential of women as a reforming force not yet fully integrated into a society largely formed by men. Day care would not maintain the status quo or extend the logic of the society to its full realization, but would in some significant ways attempt to block the present direction of society and start it off in a new one.

Perhaps this triad of views should be considered points on a spectrum rather than sharply distinct alternatives. One could conceive, for instance, of the further realization of advanced industrial society, through the admission of women and the preparation of more children, as a form of "patchwork" on a large scale, even though the patches would be coming to equal or surpass the original garment. On the other hand, the drive toward full realization of the society's logic, whether conceived simply in terms of fulfilling the "American Dream" or more strictly in terms of extending the technical rationality of industrialism into areas which have eluded it, suggests a kind of utopian effort (some might consider it a negative utopia); and it becomes hard to draw a line between those reforms, of the family, for example, which promise the "same" society to the nth degree and those which promise something not only new but basically different. Finally, this triad does not imply some kind of normative hierarchy. Within each category will be found those whose attitudes toward day care is more or less well thought out, or more or less self-serving.

I

The patchwork view, to begin, has dominated the rationale for day care since the establishment of the first "day nurseries" a century ago. That view was reinforced after World War I by the influx of professional social workers into what had been the domain, and a rather flourishing one, too, of amateur "day nursery ladies." Where these amateurs had been unimaginative enough to treat day care as a relatively straightforward response to economic hardship, the professionals regarded the application for day care as an indication of "maladjustment" and a sign of the family's need for extensive casework. It was repeatedly asserted that day care, like patchwork, was only a temporary expedient, with the pious hope that it would be rendered unnecessary by improved family or social conditions.[3]

If the renewed interest in day care hardly suggests a phenomenon about to disappear, neither does it suggest that the patchwork view has any fewer adherents. They might be divided, however, by what it is they primarily hope to patch: the tax rolls, touched and in some cases strained by never popular welfare costs; the economic duress of poor families, especially the female-headed families who constitute such an imposing percentage of the welfare population; or the emotional and intellectual deprivation of children in such homes.

Day care, it should be understood, has been and continues to be closely connected with welfare. At the local level, the intake procedures and the financing of day care centers have been intertwined with the work of the welfare department. Welfare departments are always under pressure to put recipients to work, and in some cases day care has provided a means of pressuring welfare mothers to take jobs, although the scarcity of day-care space has meant that, in fact, there may have been far more welfare mothers desiring to work but unable to do so because day care was not available than welfare mothers forced to work because it was. At least until the present.

But the expansion of day-care services has been spurred by federally assisted work-training programs for welfare mothers as well as by a growing public realization that the welfare rolls are not filled with "able-bodied men." Day care has become an essential ingredient of welfare reform plans. Whether it will help combine the needs and desires of welfare mothers concerning work and child care so that they truly can better themselves economically, or whether it will be aimed primarily at cutting welfare costs, providing only minimal care so as to assuage consciences uneasy about pressuring mothers of young children to take jobs, is yet to be seen.

Three separate efforts at day-care legislation exemplify the great differences which can exist within the patchwork category.

1. The Nixon Administration's welfare reform bill calls for extensive day care facilities within a few years' time. Mothers of school age children could be obliged to use these and take available jobs or lose all welfare assistance—an aspect of the reform which has disturbed observers familiar with the abuse of work requirements at the local level. Their concern has been justified by Federal approval of pilot projects in California, Illinois, and New York which would force welfare mothers even of pre-school children either to take jobs or to care for the children of other welfare mothers who are working; a measure, say the critics, raising serious problems of family rights as well as of the quality of care these children might be receiving.

2. Senator Russell Long, chairman of the Senate Finance Committee, has introduced a bill (Child Care Services Act, S. 2003) that would create a Day-Care Corporation to lend money to local groups who wishes to provide day care.[4] His bill is thought to stand little chance of passage, but since he is chairman of the Senate Finance Committee other day-care bills will pass through his hands for funding. If his own bill is any indication he seems to favor strong work requirements in exchange for day-care funding, little community control over day-care centers, and a minimum of Federal expenditure, without which there can be no quality day care. While Long's bill has the attractive feature of raising the income level for sliding scale fees and the income tax deduction for child care, the day-care centers would be largely funded by

parent-paid fees, almost certainly resulting in custodial centers with minimum standards for staff ratio and programming.

3. The Comprehensive Child Development Program (Title V of the Economic Opportunity Amendments of 1971) emerged from a House-Senate conference reconciliation of bills introduced by Senator Walter Mondale and Representative John Brademas and passed by the Senate and House respectively. The measure, approved by Congress and then vetoed by President Nixon, was meant to fulfill the stated aims of the Administration's welfare reform program by freeing women on relief as well as assisting the "working poor" to move into the economic mainstream. But the bill went beyond work-oriented economic patchwork to offer another justification and organizing concept for day care, namely child development. The first hope was to break the "poverty cycle": if children were given good medical care, sound nutrition, and a stimulating environment in their earliest, most impressionable years, then perhaps wide-spread retardation, medical problems, and school failure might not handicap the children presently condemned to becoming second- and third-generation welfare recipients.[5]

The intent of the Mondale-Brademas bill was, in fact, a radical departure from previous government attitudes toward early childhood services. The legislation still provided free or subsidized services largely to disadvantaged families (but including the "working poor"), but the bill's language and provisions were concerned with nothing less than providing "every child with a fair and full opportunity to reach his full potential . . . ." In rationale, then, it expressed the realization view of day care as much as the patchwork, suggesting that not only the special cases but the average child as well must be guaranteed superior child care. "The bill is as American as apple pie," declared Senator Alan Cranston during Senate debate, comparing the measure with the American tradition of public education. Day care, in this case, becomes not merely a means of repairing anomalies but a next step in the evolution of society.

The fact that Title V was a new departure was firmly admitted, even exaggerated, in the President's veto message, which cited it as grounds for the measure's rejection. "For the Federal Government to plunge headlong financially into supporting child development would commit the vast moral authority of the National Government to the side of communal approaches to child rearing over against the family-centered approach." By declaring that the need for the comprehensive program had not been demonstrated, that it duplicated in part his own welfare reform efforts, that it was too expensive, that its decentralized local control features left no role for the state governments, and that it might "diminish both parental authority and parental involvement with children," the President signalled his own more strictly patchwork view of day care as an unfortunate but necessary deviation from American norms, a minimal effort associated with the poor and public relief.

Allied to the Mondale-Brademas approach to child care, and similarly straddling the patchwork and realization notions, is the work of numerous educators and psychologists in child development.

Attention to early child development has been part of educational baggage for well over a century (Pestalozzi, Frobel, Montessori) if not longer (Mill, Rousseau). Frobel and Montessori even ejoyed a short-lived popularity in the United States before World War I, but it is only since World War II that such thinking has had a large scale impact here. The work of the Swiss psychologist Jean Piaget and the American psychologists Jerome Bruner and J. McViker Hunt has had a tremendous influence in pointing out the early and rapid cognitive development of children long before the age of five or six, when they traditionally begin school. From its first day an infant begins to learn, to construct theories, to have expectations about other people's behavior, and by the age of two has, as Noam Chomsky showed, reinvented the basic grammatical and syntatical rules of his language. Such scientific work is the basis for many of the changing attitudes toward children, child-rearing, and pre-school education.[7]

For a variety of historical and social reasons it has been difficult to put these theories to work. Thinking about the infant and small child has been governed until recently by Freudian analysts; the work of such people as Anna Freud and John Bowlby, with their emphasis on the affective relationship between mother and child, has supported the prevalent American prejudice against the mother of young children leaving their care to mother substitutes or day-care centers and nursery schools.[8] About the best one was able to do by way of providing for child development in any formal way was to send a child to a nursery school from the age of three, and at that only for a half-day. This was a course almost exclusively open to those who could pay stiff tuition fees, and therefore almost universally closed to the poor.[9]

Until the early sixties, when Montessori was re-introduced into the United States and some of Piaget's theories began to be circulated, even these nursery schools could be considered little more than play schools. Whatever day-care centers existed operated in much the same way in terms of educational offerings. All this changed radically in the sixties. The beginning of Headstart in 1965 helped more than any other single factor to publicize these child development theories and popularize the importance of early childhood learning.

In addressing its program primarily to what were described as "culturally disadvantaged" children, Headstart inspired a number of programs and techniques especially addressed to the needs of children from deprived environments. From this perspective Headstart has been directed largely to patchwork efforts—to giving children a "head start" in their primary school years, compensating for the apparent inability of public schools to teach, educate, or understand the non-Anglo or non-middle-class child. For the same reasons pre-school education has come to seem an attractive addition to day care. The hope that potential school non-achievers, with the proper intellectual, emotional, and social stimulation, will improve their chances in school is a politically attractive counter-balance to the considerable cost of adding effective education programs to day-care centers.

It is hard to dispute the aims of the patchwork approach to day care. But it is less difficult to wonder whether these aims will be accomplished and to point out the ways in which different patchwork approaches work against one another. To begin with, day care is expensive. The cost per child of full care in a day-care center was estimated at $1,245 a year in 1967 for *minimum* care —that which was "essential to maintaining the health and safety of the child, but with relatively little attention to his developmental needs." A "desirable" program replete with individual developmental activities was estimated at $2,320 per child. In fact, the present makeshift care arranged by working mothers or welfare mothers in work-training programs averages less than $500 a year in cost, when it is done for remuneration at all.[10]

Those who imagine day care as a cheap instrument for getting women off welfare rolls are apt to be disappointed—or else to support extremely minimal care, in which case unconscionable pressures on mothers to surrender child-rearing to institutions they distrust may be the outcome. Such minimal care, of course, runs directly against the intentions of those who see day care as providing a health and education environment presently not available in poor homes. Nor are funds the only question mark.

Jerome Bruner, Director of Harvard's Center for Cognitive Studies, who more than any other scholar and researcher gave the theoretical underpinnings to early childhood education in the U.S., has recently taken a cautious position regarding the present state of developmental studies and their potential for day-care programming. He made special note of the problems that white, middle-class social scientists have in seeing their own theories as culture-bound and therefore subject to some of the criticism that Blacks, Chicanos, and Puerto Ricans have made about Headstart and other compensatory education programs.[11] In testimony before the Mondale Committee, Evelyn Moore, Director of the Black Child Development Institute, took a strong critical stance against the research provisions of the Comprehensive Child Development Act on the grounds that past efforts have had little program effect and that they inevitably end—because of language, project design, and white, middle-class perceptions—in demeaning the black child.[13] Indeed, scientific respect for cultural pluralism may be hard to attain in developing educational programs for day care. In the same volume in which Jerome Bruner takes a critical look at early childhood studies, Jerome Kagan, his counter part at Yale, began an article on "Cognitive Development and Programs for Day Care" with the following observation:

> Most Americans believe that young children should: 1) feel loved and valued by the adults who care for him, develop trust in, and affection and respect for those adults, so that in the future the child will 2) develop an autonomous identity and believe that he can determine his own actions and decide what he alone should believe, 3) be free of fear and anxiety and be able to enjoy life, 4) develop his intellectual capacities to the fullest and perform with competence on those problems society presents to him.[13]

At first glance such a supposed consensus may seem unexceptionable, although even a casual observer might note a certain middle-class, professional tone to the language (which could simply be accepted as Kagan's way of putting what others might express differently). The fact is that, even in such generalities as these, the problem is greater than one of tone. Though many Americans would agree in theory that their children should develop an "autonomous identity" (it sounds up-to-date, after all), in practice they have something else in mind. And other Americans would not even grant the point in theory. For them children should *not* believe they can determine their own actions or individually decide what to believe. Nor is developing "intellectual capacities to the fullest" necessarily such a clearly held ideal in a situation where other capacities—social, athletic, etc.—may compete for attention. Any reader of Herbert Gans' *Urban Villagers* knows that many Italians, to name one relatively intact ethnic group, think there are community values more important than "autonomous identity." These are not quibbles, for people operating programs can sadly learn that "autonomous identity" translates very differently from culture to culture and class to class.[14]

Nor is the absence of commonly agreed upon child-rearing values the last difficulty facing day-care programmers. Trained personnel for day-care programs are also in short supply. The day-care provisions foreseen under the 1967 Work Incentive Program foundered on this very point. "Directors and head teachers are so scarce that problems of financing and licensing would seem small next to lack of staff," read one report on the program.[15]

The basic problem faced by the patchwork approach is that in our society quality services, whether in medicine, transportation, or schooling, are more likely to be available to the middle class than to the poor, even when subsidized. The Mondale-Brademas legislation, like the Family Assistance Plan, has attempted to obtain wider support for better services by including the working poor along with the welfare poor in its consideration, and indeed the Mondale bill has received enthusiastic backing from the AFL-CIO. The patchwork use of day care today differs from its earlier version, which asserted that the ideal was always the mother in the home. The new version springs, partially, from a great suspicion that the lower-class family is a defective socializing agent for children. But the fallout from changing attitudes toward work, home, and day care, in combination with the expansion of *quality* services and the change in ideology, may yet, as in so many other cases, limit the poor to the "trickle-down" from the more affluent.

While Headstart has been directed toward patchwork efforts its underlying impetus and that of most early learning research is clearly concerned with the goals of realization, of pushing present tendencies along their logical course, toward equal opportunity for

all members of American society to make it through the educational system—a process which has become the single most important standard for judging whether people are employable and
prepared to fit into a rapidly evolving technological society. Maya
Pines in *Revolution in Learning* realistically assesses the expectation of most pre-school educators when she writes:

> The pioneers of early learning want to give every child a chance to develop
> his capacities to the fullest. Their techniques will increase man's variety,
> not reduce it. If they succeed, middle-class children will no longer be held
> back to some comfortable average—and poor children will no longer be
> crushed before they can learn to learn. Both will be allowed to find their
> own intellectual identities. Both still come closer to reaching their poten-
> tial. This should make each human life more interesting, more productive,
> and more rewarding.[16]

II

We have already seen the tendency of some legislators and
educators to treat day care as a normal, not merely a remedial ad-
vance in American society. This view of day care as a natural
realization of the society's direction also gets support from working women, some industrial and franchise day-care services, and an
important segment of the women's liberation movement. At one
end of the spectrum marked by this category, working women—
some 4.5 million of them have children under six—simply seek a
satisfactory solution for a problem which less and less can be
handled by family and friends and more and more is viewed as a
normal part of economic life. At the other end, futurists imagine
our "super-industrialism" logically issuing not only in day care but
in "professional parenthood":

> Raising children, after all, requires skills that are by no means univer-
> sal. We don't let "just anyone" perform brain surgery. . . . Yet we allow
> virtually anyone . . . to try his or her hand at raising young human be-
> ings. . . . the greatest single preserve of the amateur.
>
> As the present system cracks and the super-industrial revolution rolls
> over us . . . we can expect vociferous demands for an end to parental dilet-
> tantism . . . . professional parenthood is certain to be proposed, if only
> because it fits so perfectly with the society's overall push toward speciali-
> zation. . . . Even now millions of parents, given the opportunity, would
> happily relinquish their parental responsibilities—and not necessarily
> through irresponsibility or lack of love. Harried, frenzied, up against a
> wall, they have come to see themselves as inadequate to the tasks. Given
> affluence and the existence of specially equipped and licensed professional

parents, many of today's parents would not only gladly surrender their children to them, but would look upon it as an act of love, rather than rejection.[17]

Among the more workaday efforts to adjust the demands of child care to the demands of full employment for women are industrial and franchise day-care centers. A few manufacturing and service organizations with a high percentage of women employees have expressed interest in or have actually established day-care centers. Such centers, it is argued, will help provide a stable work force, reduce tardiness and absenteeism, and increase the level of production by insuring working mothers "peace of mind." So far, however, interest—on the part of workers, unions, and the companies themselves—has far outrun action. Many companies are hesitant to expand fringe benefits in the direction of day care. The New York Bell Telephone Company, despite union pressure, has expressed great reluctance to initiate day-care for its employees, although it has a 70% staff turnover every year. They cite as reasons cost, lack of adequate space, and the fact that mothers would have to travel during the rush hour with small children. On the other hand, Illinois Bell Telephone has taken a step in assisting its employees by setting up a day care staff that helps employees find day-care homes in their own neighborhoods. The company gives no financial aid aside from staff expenses toward day care.[18] Other industries, including KLH in Cambridge, Avco in Boston, and Tioga Sportswear in Fall River, Massachusetts, have opened centers to provide day care for their employees. If these pioneering companies succeed in proving that day care will indeed cut employee turnover, tardiness, and absenteeism and increase production, then it could become as commonplace for a factory to have a day-care center as a cafeteria.

A related development is franchise day care, sometimes referred to as "Kentucky Fried Children." Franchise centers, which must be able to make a profit, are a riskier operation than industrial centers; many observers feel that the future of such operations will depend on the availability of government funds and welfare reform. On the other hand, industrial and franchise day care may end by addressing different population groups, although the result will be the same: easier entry of women into the labor market. Industrial centers will largely serve a population of semiskilled and skilled "blue-collar women"—telephone operators, factory operators, hospital staff, clerks, etc. Franchise centers are more likely to serve a population of white-collar women—teachers, executives, professionals. They could therefore charge sufficiently high fees, probably stressing in return the "latest" in early-learning techniques for an appreciative middle- and upper-class clientele.

Low-income working women and welfare mothers tend to see quality day care as supportive of their family situation, a means of keeping the family intact and functioning while a mother either becomes a primary or absolutely necessary secondary bread-winner. The feminist movement does not challenge such an out-look, and most feminist literature tries to keep the interests of low-income and welfare women in mind; but feminists' hopes for day care certainly go beyond the income question. For them, day care offers a means of encouraging basic social changes, changes with which low-income and poor women are not necessarily in agreement.

Women's Liberation is, of course, an extremely diverse move-ment, but the National Organization for Women (NOW) probably represents the broadest consensus. Like other women's liberation groups it has emerged from the general American Left; hence its demands are couched as sharp criticisms of the nation's status quo. Nonetheless, NOW's aims appear more directed at *opening up* the present economic structures to women than at challenging those structures. While NOW has learned from the tactics of black mil-itancy, its philosophical attitude toward U.S. society, if we may draw an analogy to the racial situation, is still more integrationist than separatist or revolutionary. Its thinking tends in the direction of encouraging women to adopt the qualifications and orientation of the male-dominated work ethic. Its three major demands (abor-tion on demand; free 24-hour day care; equal pay for equal work) are directly related to freeing women from their sex-role occupa-tions and allowing them to participate equally with men in the labor market. It is interesting to note that two of the three de-mands are concerned with motherhood and only one with the situation at the workplace. Day care is a crucial ingredient in a view of women's liberation which focuses on "integrating" present economic structures. It does not simply propose that women should have equal child-rearing responsibilities with men (which could be accomplished a number of other ways, e.g., a shorter work week); rather it proposes that women should have no greater child-rearing responsibilities than do men *in our present society*.

Day care, in effect, would fulfill the functions women presently fill.[19]

Other feminists like Eva Figes and Shulamith Firestone are more radical in their predictions that present pressures on the family are, and should be, only preliminaries to its total withering away, or at least its transformation into an entirely egalitarian and non-permanent form of compansionship.

Shulamith Firestone in *The Dialectic of Sex* has pushed the logic of anatomy-ought-not-to-be-destiny to its extreme conclusions and described the ultimate revolution as one in which the feminist and the cybernetic revolution will have joined to create a new paradise on earth, which would include "1. the freeing of women from the tyranny of their biology by any means available [including artificial reproduction], and the diffusion of the childbearing and childrearing role to the society as a whole, to men and other children as well as women; 2. the economic independence and self-determination of all [including children] and 3. the total integration of women and children into the larger society." In the society which she foresees there would be no necessary sex or economic roles for individuals. Thus the family would become superfluous; children would belong to everyone and be cared for by everyone. Interestingly enough, in the short term Firestone sees day-care centers as they are now constituted as a means of taking pressure off women and thereby undermining their revolutionary consciousness: "Day-care centers buy women off."[20]

Eva Figes in *Patriarchal Attitudes* is equally forthright in her prediction that, one way or the other, marriage will disappear: "Either one goes on liberalizing the divorce laws, until marriage stands exposed as a hollow sham . . . or one takes a short cut and abolishes marriage altogether. . . . Women must be treated as total human beings in their own right. . . . Children must be treated as primarily the property of the state. . . . This means fairly substantial child allowances for all children, and sufficient state and/or industrial nurseries for children."[21]

Firestone's and Figes' positions would certainly be labelled "utopian" by most of the public, if harsher language were not employed. Firestone without question, and possibly Figes, and surely many other feminists themselves consider such proposals "radical" and "utopian." But it is just as reasonable to consider them under the "day care as realization" heading: they regard day care as part of a process in which the autonomy and freedom of action of the individual, woman or child, is the overriding goal. Their views seem to be further extensions of an affluent, technologically advanced, production-oriented society which puts relatively little value on contemplation, permanency, tradition, or community.

Some radical feminists, opposed to the family though they may be, nonetheless recongize that its passing would not guarantee a society very different from the one they contest. Linda Gordon, a Marxist feminist, points out that "If it were clever enough . . . the system could survive the destruction of the family."

> The system gave us the vote and equal rights, and it still exploits us all, woman and man. The system could give us equal wages, equal education, and could probably provide day-care centers and jobs for us all. . . .
>
> In contemporary society men and women could be equal—equally harnessed to the demands of consumption, technology and imperialism. . . . Child care could be given over to large nurseries and schools (probably still run by women), as well adapted families to the task of brainwashing children. . . . Women could win the freedom to produce children only at will, with partners (or injections) of their choice, and with state-provided facilities for their care, without making themselves whole human beings.[22]

She goes on to comment, "Some of these nightmares may not be so fantastic." In certain strata of society the breakdown of the family is well underway. This development is "objectively revolutionary" but not, the author adds, "entirely desirable . . . nor do we think its outcome predetermined."[23]

III

It would be unfair, however, to suggest that women's liberation, in looking upon day care as an instrument for modifying the whole family structure, is concerned solely with achieving economic freedom for mothers. According to feminists, the nuclear family is a good place neither for women to spend their lives nor for children to grow up: the nuclear family, one might say, is not healthy for children or other living things. Thus, in concluding that "quality child-care programs are good for children," NOW argues that

> Young children need peer relationships, additional adult models, enriched educational programs, particularly true because half of the intellectual development of a child is achieved by age 4. . . . A child socialized by one whose human role is limited, essentially, to motherhood may be proportionately deprived of varied learning experiences. In a circular fashion, the

development of children has been intimately influenced by the development of women.[24]

Although the rest of the NOW statement reads like that of any parent group demanding the "best for our children," it does introduce a certain utopian element in its suggestion that a generation of children reared outside the grasp of oppressed women would be significantly enriched in learning and experience. And generally an emphasis on the "children's liberation" aspect of day care marks the utopian approach to the issue. Collective child-rearing has been a common feature of utopian schemes throughout history. In the American context it has been seen as one way to mitigate traits thought undesirable in the American character: competitiveness, selfishness, violence, intolerance, acquisitiveness. Such views are current today in the American commune movement—but are not limited to it. One day-care licensing official remarked, in an interview, that he saw day care as a means of creating a cooperative, non-authoritarian society. Children would be changed by their day-care experience, learning to share, to be tolerant . . . and in changing them one would change the society regardless of its political or economic structure.

Other voices of the utopian school are less sanguine about this greening of the children and more conscious of the need to put a special stamp on day care lest it become just another prop of unredeemed society. The Radical Education Project distributes a pamphlet attacking government and industrial day care as a means of "tracking" women into low-paying jobs. "If the need for child care is isolated from other needs, women will be caught in limited reforms that will only add public to private exploitation." While maintaining women in exploitative jobs, "the day care centers will also train children to be docile, obedient workers that the system needs."[25]   Another women's liberation document, making a similar case, provides an excellent statement of the utopian attitude. "We think it is a mistake to view day care solely as an issue of women's liberation. We would like to assert that day care centers in which children are raised in groups by men and women could be as important for the liberation of children as [they] would be for the liberation of women. Group child care has a radical potential through its impact on young children."[26]

Historically, the paper argues, day care has been a function of the need for women in the labor force; if it has emerged slowly in the United States, that is only due to the belief that young children and mothers belong at home. The women's liberation movement is rejecting this latter ideology, but "the movement's present demand parallels the historical attitudes toward day care in its non-child centered approach." The paper accuses the "majority of existing U.S. day care centers" of being "glorified babysitting services," teaching children passivity, programming them through routine, and instructing them in an "invisible curriculum" of attitudes toward work, race, sex roles, competition, and cooperation.

Day care poses the problem of sharply conflicting value systems; and radicals, the paper states, should limit their demands to "space and money" while running their own centers themselves. The precise ways in which the radical center would be different are illustrated with examples concerning sex roles—the treatment of the "housekeeping corner," the presence of men teachers and the like—and the paper concludes: "Although women will benefit from a good day care program, in the final analysis their liberation depends on a total transformation of society. However, the radical restructuring of one institution (child care) can help to transform the society, for the way that children develop is a part of that transformation."[27]

The Russian and Israeli child-care systems have naturally been of special interest to those who see day care as a means of instilling radically new values. The kibbutzim and children's collectives are seen as evidence not only that group rearing of children and multiple mothering are not psychologically harmful but also that group child care could be a positive and relatively fast means of introducing and reinforcing social change at the same time they provide socialization and intellectual stimulation.

Urie Bronfenbrenner, a student of Russian child care practices, has supported day care as a means for freeing women—presumably not simply disadvantaged ones—from the isolation and "drudgery" of the nuclear family system. In that regard, Bronfenbrenner does not differ much from the "day care as realization" approach. However, he makes much of the importance of parent participation in day care—male as well as female; and elsewhere Bronfenbrenner has elaborated a new approach toward childrearing in the United States which reveals sharp differences in emphasis with women's liberation spokeswomen who are primarily concerned with granting mothers economic independence. Bronfenbrenner protests the segregation of children from adult activities and the "real world." He would restructure community, school, and work life to break down the barriers between play, education, and productive work, and between the assigned roles of men and women, of children, employed adults, and the aged. Bronfenbrenner is clearly proposing the family and child-rearing as the fulcrum for shifting American values and institutions in a utopian direction.[28]

Bronfenbrenner's proposals do not depend strictly on his study of Soviet child-rearing. But the relevance of the Russian and Israeli examples is a problem in any case. The primary feature of their child-care systems, after all, is that they are only part of a radical, conscious, and planned system for social change within the whole society. They exist in a national and ideological context quite different from anything in the United States.

In general, the utopian approach to day care is far stronger in intention than in program. Government and industrial co-optation is feared; the desire to create a different sort of child is announced, but insofar as the method to this end is described, it seems like rather minor variations on the techniques of other day-care programs. (This is not true of Bronfenbrenner, of course, whose innovations are less within the day care center itself than in the patterns of employment, school, and local community, which he would restyle in order to integrate children with other age groups and with adult activities.) Even the utopian goals are stated rather vaguely. Bettye Caldwell, whose work in Syracuse has convinced her of the vast possibilities of truly early learning in infant day-care centers, has criticized all approaches in this regard.

> With our tradition of valuing rugged individualism, we have been reluctant to say much about the kinds of children we want. Do we want obedient children? Happy children? Adaptive children? Children who remain faithful to the values of their families? Militant children? Bright children? Group-oriented children? Woodstock and Maypole youth or Peace Corps youth? Eventual adults who can slip from one type to another? . . .
>
> At this moment in history, when we are on the threshold of embarking on a nationwide program of social intervention offered through comprehensive child care, we let ourselves prattle about such things as cost per child, physical facilities, or even community control. And when we begin to think big about what kinds of children we want to have in the next generation, about which human characteristics will stand them in good stead in a world changing so rapidly, we fall back on generalities such as care and protection.[29]

Perhaps what Bettye Caldwell considers a failure of nerve is an understandable modesty before the somewhat awesome task she proposes: thinking big "about what kinds of children we want to have in the next generation." But it is interesting that not even among those who oppose the present direction of society is much of such "thinking big" done.

IV

Day-care services are going to be expanded. If nothing else, the broad range of forces desiring day care practically guarantees Federal funding of some sort. But the same combination of forces may produce unexpected results. Two examples will suffice.

1. A conflict exists between the patchwork outlook, which foresees a large but still limited constituency for day care, and the realization outlook, which foresees day care (and the working mother) as part of the normal pattern of American family life. The former may determine the funding of day care while the latter, increasingly accepted, may determine the demand. The consequence of a demand which far outstrips the supply will be custodial care, or educational care which could easily duplicate the mistakes of the urban school systems.

2. Another possibility is that the "realization" and "utopia" views may be less influential in accomplishing their own aims than in unwittingly reinforcing the ability of some patchworkers to force welfare mothers to leave their children in day care and take jobs against their will. Ironically, the "mother at home" sterotype which women's liberation understandably criticizes has also been an uncertain but nonetheless real protection for welfare mothers against the dictates of local authorities. And if the support given day care by women's liberation, both in its "realization" and "utopia" branches, may prove all too congruent with the aims of the penny-pinching version of patchwork, on the issue of the family it is theoretically at odds with the more generous version of patchwork day care. The latter envisions day care as part of a welfare reform program with the ultimate end of strengthening the family unit. Women's liberation, on the other hand, has envisioned day care as part of the process of loosening or even dissolving the family unit. Patchwork theorists see day care as a step forward enabling families, especially female-headed ones, to finally take responsibility themselves for their children's upkeep rather than have it be a (poorly borne) state burden. Many "realization" and "utopia"

supporters of day care, however, see it at least partially as a trans-
ferral of responsibility for children to the state.

One can imagine other conflicts and convergences among the
presently united day-care front that may lead to unintended consequences—and one ought to. Those who believe in the great
potential of day care would be wise to indulge in a little futurism,
speculating on the books to be written twenty years hence
chronicling the controversies and disappointments surrounding the
national day-care system. For a starter, how about *Day Care and
Sex Education?*

NOTES

1. Representative Bella Abzug (D., N.Y.), for example, has called for 24-
   hour child-care centers to be funded at the rate of ten billion dollars
   annually by the end of the 1970's *(New York Times,* February 23, 1971).
2. Boston, 1971.
3 There is no real history of the over one hundred years of day care in
   America, a lack we hope will be remedied in a forthcoming book on day
   care by Peggy Steinfels.
4. *Material Related to Child Care Legislation: Description of S. 2003,* Senate
   Committee on Finance, 92nd Cong., 1st sess., 1971, pp. 39-47.
5. *Comprehensive Child Development Act of 1971: Hearings on S.1512,*
   Senate Subcommittee on Children and Youth, 92nd Cong., 1st sess.,
   1971, pp. 3-55; and *H.R. 6748: A Bill to Provide a Comprehensive Child
   Development Act,* 92nd Cong., 1st sess.
6. *Hearings on S.1512,* p. 3.
7. For examples of this work see Fred M. Hechinger, ed., *Pre-School Education Today* (New York, 1966), and Maya Pines, *Revolution in Learning:
   The Years from Birth to Six* (New York, 1970).
8. Bettye M. Caldwell, "A Timid Giant Grows Bolder," *Saturday Review,*
   February 20, 1971, p. 49; John Bowlby, *Maternal Care and Mental
   Health;* and Margaret Mead et al., *Deprivation of Mental Care: A Reassessment of Its Effects* (New York, 1967).
9. A recent study of pre-school education by the United States Office of
   Education suggests that this picture may have changed somewhat. Among
   children age three and four, the percentage of black children enrolled in
   pre-school programs (14.4 and 30.9) was slightly higher than the percentage of white children (12.6 and 27.1) *(New York Times,* October 5,
   1971).
10. *Material Related to Child Care Legislation,* pp. 11-12.
11. U.S. Office of Economic Opportunity, *Day Care: Resources for Deci-
    sions,* 1971, pp. 91-94.
12. *Hearings on S.1512,* pp. 366-371.
13. *Day Care: Resources for Decisions,* p. 136.
14. For example, the Amalgamated Clothing Workers Union at its Chicago
    day-care center found that the center's policy of "no corporal punish-
    ment for misconduct . . . often raises conflict with the parents, who are

more accustomed to responding to misconduct or conflict with a more severe or physical means of punishment" (*Hearings on S. 1512*, p. 484).

15. *Material Related to Child Care Legislation*, p. 14; see also Jule Sugarman's testimony, *Hearings on S.1512*, p. 167.

16. Pines, p. 272.

17. Alvin Toffler, *Future Shock* (New York, 1970), pp. 215-216.

18. *New York Times*, October 29, 1970; Illinois Bell Employees' House Organ, n.d.

19. To be exact, a statement of the NOW Task Force on Child Care, "Why Feminists Want Child Care," declares: "NOW believes that the care and welfare of children is incumbent on society *and* parents. We reject the idea that mothers have a special child care role that is not to be shared equally by fathers. Men need the humanizing experiences of nurturance and guidance of another human organism." The concrete proposals in the statement, however, deal only with day care and not at all with enlarging the present child-rearing role of fathers.

20. Shulamith Firestone, *The Dialectic of Sex* (New York, 1971), pp. 238-240.

21. Eva Figes, *Patriarchial Attitudes* (Greenwich, Conn., 1970), p. 179.

22. Linda Gordon, "Functions of the Family," *Voices from Women's Liberation* (New York, 1971), pp. 186-187.

23. These phrases are from Linda Gordon's pamphlet *Families* (Cambridge, Mass., 1970), pp. 23-24. The ending to the pamphlet is essentially the same as that of the article cited above, with a few changes in wording.

24. "Why Feminists Want Child Care."

25. Vicki Breitbart, "Day Care, Who Cares?" (Detroit, n.d.), p. 7.

26. "Day Care," a five-page mimeographed pamphlet from the Women's Center of New York, 36 W. 22nd Street, N.Y., N.Y.

27. Ibid.

28. Urie Bronfenbrenner, *Two Worlds of Childhood* (New York, 1970), pp. 152-166; *New York Times* March 28, 1971, an interview with Bronfenbrenner; and "Children and Parents: Together in the World," Report of Forum 15, 1970 White House Conference on Children (working copy).

29. Caldwell, pp. 65-66.

THE NEW HOMESTEADING MOVEMENT: FROM UTOPIA TO EUTOPIA

MAYNARD KAUFMAN

> ... for, as Professor Patrick Geddes points out, Sir Thomas More was an inveterate punster, and Utopia is a mockname for either Outopia, which means no-place, or Eutopia—the good place.
>
> —Lewis Mumford, *The Story of Utopias* (1922), p. 267.

WHILE IT MAY NOT SOUND as though there is much difference between "utopia" and "eutopia," it is the theme of this essay that there is now a definite movement from "no-place" to "the good place" which is significant for what it reveals about the quest for the good life in America and important as an expression of the counter culture. This is the new homesteading movement, or the back-to-the-land movement, associated with agrarian communes and with the vogue for organic foods and gardening. Urban intellectuals have condemned this movement as a cop-out and warned against its atavistic tendency; they have derided its primitivism and denied the possibility of a subsistence economy. Perhaps such negative attitudes are justified; perhaps they reflect urban provincialism. In any event, judgments about a social phenomenon, if they are not to be merely pejorative, should be well-informed; and thus, even though I think this movement stands in need of support and encouragement at this time, my main purpose here is to mediate a better understanding of these new homesteaders and their motivations.

Critics of the homesteading movement seem to assume that it is a visionary and impractical dream in our highly industrialized so-

Maynard Kaufman was born on a farm in South Dakota and received his graduate education at the University of Chicago Divinity School. He now lives on a farm and teaches in the Religion Department of Western Michigan University at Kalamazoo, Michigan.

ciety—that it is indeed "utopian." We shall see that such criticism is partly true, but it misses the important fact that as the utopian vision finds a local habitation, after the seeking is done and a good place is found, the practical problems of living on the land must be mastered. Thus the full title of a recent book is *The Ex-urbanite's Complete & Illustrated Easy-Does-It First-Time Farmer's Guide, A Useful Book.*[1] The literature which is generated by (and in turn helps to generate) the new homesteading movement consists almost entirely of practical, how-to-do-it information. Periodicals such as *The Mother Earth News, Countryside,* and *The Green Revolution* are unofficial organs of the movement, while *Organic Gardening and Farming* has very recently discovered the proximity of its back-to-nature agriculture to the new back-to-the-land movement. The several editions of *The Whole Earth Catalog*, with its unique mixture of futurism and nostalgia, humanized technology and old-time tools and crafts, are also useful to the new homesteader.

This movement differs from the older homesteading movement of the 1930's in that it is not as strongly stimulated by an economic depression. The newer homesteaders are also less theoretical, less inclined to justify and rationalize their intention to "live off the land." Earlier drop-outs, such as Scott Nearing and Ralph Borsodi,[2] were social scientists concerned to demonstrate, both statistically and in practice, the possibility of their utopian visions. Like the newer homesteaders of today, however, they were sensitive to what we now call "ecology" and to the ecological aspects of homesteading. In his book of 1929, *This Ugly Civilization*, Ralph Borsodi already envisioned a new homesteading movement as an alternative to further environmental degradation.

> To be able to abandon the buying of the products of our non-essential and undesirable factories, and still be comfortable, the home must be reorganized—it must be made into an economically creative institution. It must cease being a mere consumption unit. It must become a production unit as well. It must be as nearly as possible an organic home—house, land, machines, materials and a group of individuals organized not for mere consumption but for creative and productive living.[3]

Subsistence homesteading might thus be defined as living on a productive, self-sufficient small farm where needs and wants for boughten goods are reduced to a minimum. And we might emphasize that the aesthetic aspects of homesteading are at least as important as its economic aspects; it appeals to those who are in search of a simple, healthful, and satisfying way of life.

If the new homesteading movement is not stimulated primarily by economic necessity, it will be helpful to discern its origins and motivations. Let us try, then, to trace the movement from utopia to eutopia, even though it may require sweeping generalizations.

The utopian phase in the counter culture emerged gradually as the prevailing techno-culture became so total and all-encompassing that there was literally no place to go to escape except to drop out. Thus a "turned-off" generation becomes "down and out" instead of "up and coming," in the words of Gibson Winter, as it "embodies the antithesis of techno-man and his controlled world."[4] Having no place to go, however, the drop-out becomes, according to Winter, a mendicant who exists parasitically in the interstices of the techno-culture. He might, since he was spawned by a middle-class society that has made the manufacture of drugs a major industry, quite naturally turn to various drugs and hallucinogens to discover and explore his inner space. Such drugs are, as Gibson Winter goes on to point out, a threat to the older generation because they break up the controls that maintain the stability of the establishment: "they represent the breaking up of will, calculation and control which is the latter-day version of the Protestant ethic."[5] It is certainly true that drugs, and especially marijuana and LSD, have come to be associated with those who rebel against the techno-culture. Charles Reich claims that the widespread use of marijuana is an extremely important catalyst in precipitating a new consciousness. He points out that "in some less uptight society marijuana would be just a toy, a harmless 'high.' But in a society that keeps its citizens within a closed system of thought, that depends so much on systematic indoctrination and an imposed consciousness, marijuana is a maker of revolution, a truth-serum."[6] It would be a mistake to conclude from this that drugs are the cause of the cultural revolution or that the visions they promote serve as patterns for a new culture. Rather, just as drugs relax the controls of the prevailing techno-culture, so they are part of a larger cultural disintegration. Young people turn to drugs because they find nothing else worth doing; "doing" drugs is first a symptom of meaninglessness. Afterwards drugs may be appropriated as symbols of a new and liberated consciousness, after they have revealed the artificiality of cultural controls and thus exposed the mendacity of political and economic spokesmen.

It is important to reiterate the fact that young people "do" drugs because the socio-economic system offers them no meaningful work to do. Paul Goodman called attention to this problem (*Growing Up Absurd*) some ten years ago in relation to the dropouts of the Beat Generation. Drop-outs are far more pervasive now, of course, but perhaps the situation is more hopeful than it was ten years ago. We can now recognize that the drop-out embodies a powerful critique of the established techno-culture, and this is especially obvious as the young begin to work out alternatives to it, such as homesteading. We can also now see the transience of the drop-out phase: "doing" drugs may lead on to hard drugs and destruction, or, by means of that intensified perception the psychedelic experience offers, to a holistic or "ecological" consciousness. This, again, should not be misunderstood. Drugs are surely no magical short-cut to knowledge. Rather, the psychedelic vision is often similar to the awareness of the ecologist. As Richard Underwood put it, "both thrust one into an awareness of the inter-connectedness of things and thus a deliverance from bondage to the dichotomy of inner and outer, mind and matter, subject and object."[7] If the word "ecology" is used among young people as a symbol to express this sense of totality which includes one's own body in the balance of nature, it does not necessarily imply that those who use the word have studied this aspect of biological science. But the ecological awareness, however mediated, is most significant as an enabling factor for the development of alternatives in the counter culture. With this new awareness goes a reassessment of priorities, and the drop-out begins to seek for a way of life in harmony with his natural environment and for a sense of internal balance. He may be led to macrobiotic food, to organic food, and, of course, to organic gardening.

Some of the utopian aspects of the counter culture are opposed to the prevailing techno-culture, but others are carried over directly from it. In *The Greening of America* Charles Reich has succeeded, more than other interpreters of youth culture, in bringing its utopian elements into focus. He maintains that the new consciousness will bring with it a non-violent revolution—some time, in the future. This revolution will not negate the culture built of technology but will humanize it and thus fulfill its promise. "We have all heard the promise," explains Reich: "affluence, security, technology make possible a new life, a new permissiveness, a new freedom, a new expansion of human possibility."[8] Most of us grow up to be skeptical about this promise, but many young people, according to Reich, drop out because they feel this promise has been betrayed. Reich's revolutionary "Consciousness III" thus turns out to be a more stubbornly believed version of the kind of utopian aspiration engendered by the Industrial Revolution. (Most utopian thought today, according to Northrop Frye, includes technological themes, "and, because technology is progressive, getting to the utopia has tended increasingly to be a journey in time rather than space, a vision of the future and not of a society located in some isolated spot on the globe."[9] Reich, however, may have projected his liberal aspirations into the youth culture movement. It is more likely that the widespread use of marijuana and the concentration on "nowness" it induces has helped to expose the vacuity of an abstract future (postponed gratification) and to undercut the rhetoric of progress.

The drop-out phase among "hippies" and people of the new or counter culture is intrinsically transitional. Many of those who find it difficult to give up the gadgets and material comforts of the techno-culture eventually get a job, however meaningless it may be, and are reabsorbed by the system. But an increasing number are deeply disillusioned with utopia either in the techno-culture or outside of it ("like, man, that's nowhere"). They literally move out in search of eutopia, but in doing so they seem to move in and together as well. In his very personal but beautiful story of today's communal movements Robert Houriet describes this process.

> The first phase of the movement was *implosive*, that is, an escape from the all-pervasive influences of a plastic, fragmented mass society and a return to the primal center of being and man. In the classical utopian tradition, the commune was an island, a free space, a cultural vacuum. It was the ideal situation for spiritual revelation—for regaining the vision of a simpler, unified life and the pristine consciousness of uncomplicated, tribal man. But unlike the desert island, the communes were not naturally surrounded by an ocean to keep the "outside" society at bay. Exiles in their own country, they had to erect psychological defenses against the "outside" by drawing a "we/they" dichotomy that often verged on paranoia.[10]

The attempt to make a new beginning is almost invariably charged with the symbolism of a New Creation, Adam and Eve in Paradise, and it thus entails the substitution of an older or "classical" utopian tradition for the more recent utopian tradition. The communard may therefore be out in the wildnerness, "grooving on nature," and working out a cooperative life style that is rich in interpersonal encounters, but if he is preoccupied with fighting the society he left he has not yet appropriated the good place. He has not yet created a new community or a new social reality. The homesteader knows that freedom from the "outside" is achieved in large measure when he becomes relatively self-sufficient on the land, and very few communes have yet achieved this.

One of the basic problems which faces communards and homesteaders is to learn how to handle technology. Robert Houriet observes that "those who sought exile in communes initially rejected technology *in toto*, making little discrimination between the tools that liberated and those that enslaved. They went back to the past for tools."[11]   This is understandable in the light of the "we/they" dichotomy so pervasive in the communard's outlook, for "their" technology was to be distrusted. It was, after all, modern technology and the way of life it engendered that originally moved the communard to drop out. But at least two factors were at work to mitigate this uncompromising stand against modern technology. The first was practical; *some* modern tools and services, such as vehicles and roads, were found to be necessary, while others, such as electricity or chain saws, were useful in addition to the tools and skills of the past century. Considerations of modern technology are simply unavoidable. The other factor which led to a limited acceptance of modern technology in communes was, ironically, the ecological awareness which originally prompted the move into the country and back to nature. "All over the country," reports Robert Houriet, "communes talked enthusiastically of finding such new pollution-free sources of energy; they resurrected yellowed manuals of companies that had manufactured windmills in the 1920's, like the Le-Jay Corporation; the sent away for the designs of Pelton Wheels to harness water power; they read in *Mother Earth News* of how the methane in animal dung can be used to run electrical generators."[12]   It is here that the practical orientation of the new homesteading movement is most relevant, for it is experimenting with ecologically sound alternatives to polluting forms of technology and to agribusiness, that bastard produced when farming was raped by the chemical industry.

There are indications that the new homesteaders will soon move beyond enthusiasm and superficial know-how to a deeper understanding and to a more scientific knowledge of their place in the ecosystem. Recent issues of *Organic Gardening and Farming*

magazine include a "back to the land" section and greater emphasis on organic farming. In doing so it is moving beyond the
interests of the back-yard hobby gardener to a recognition that
organic gardening implies an organic way of life. The magazine's
association with the New Alchemy Institute could be a hopeful
sign too, for, as its director, John H. Todd, writes, "the tending
and planting of ecologically sophisticated farms will require far
more training, knowledge and labor than is now the lot of employees in specialized agribusinesses."[13]   Thus the function of the
New Alchemy Institute, says Todd, is to develop a "New Science"
for the organic homestead.

> The basic axiom of organic gardening, namely the creation of superb soils
> and the raising of high quality plants and animals, together in sophisticated
> polyculture schemes which imitate the processes of nature, will be em-
> phasized. These farms will be totally unlike the farms that the Department
> of Agriculture promotes. They will not be the large, unstable monoculture
> enterprises which are so highly specialized that they often carry out only a
> single function. The organic farms of tomorrow will no longer be geared to
> displacing people from the land, but will reverse the trend by providing
> beautiful places to live for the people who tend and love the landscapes.[14]

From this statement we can infer that the difference between the
new homesteading movement and commercial farming is equivalent to what Aldo Leopold called the "A-B cleavage": "one group
(A) regards the land as soil, and its function as commodity-produc-
tion; another group (B) regards the land as biota, and its function
as something broader."[15]   The new homesteader's romantic enthusiasm for getting back to the land and merging with it will very
likely inhibit his tendency to exploit it. The farmer may be a
conscientious steward in his use of the land, and many farmers
surely are, but the image appropriate to the homesteader's attitude
toward the land is husbandry rather than stewardship.

Is the affective or non-rational bias of the new homesteader an
asset or a liability? The situation today is very similar to that
projected by Kurt Vonnegut, Jr., in his futuristic novel of 1952,
Player Piano. His slightly rebellious anti-hero, Paul Proteus, longs
to escape from the rational and electronically automated world in
which he is an elite manager.

> Farming—now *there* was a magic word. Like so many words with a little
> magic from the past still clinging to them, the word "farming" was a
> reminder of what rugged stock the present generation had come from, of
> how tough a thing a human being could be if he had to. The word had
> little meaning in the present. There were no longer farmers, but only
> agricultural engineers.[16]

When Doctor Proteus sees his old-fashioned farm for the first time he is captivated by it. "With each new inconvenience, the place became more irresistible. It was completely isolated backwater, cut off from the boiling rapids of history, society, and the economy. Timeless."[17] Vonnegut apparently wrote to expose what he regarded as the futility and atavism of his hero's longing. The fact is that farms like the one described appeal to the new homesteaders of today for precisely the same reasons alluded to by Vonnegut, but because today's homesteaders emerged after a drop-out phase during which they learned to do without the gadgets and conveniences of our techno-culture, they can get along on the marginal land and buildings which today's agriculture abandons. And, as Robert Houriet explains, many of these drop-outs are, like Vonnegut's Paul Proteus, former affluent suburbanites.

> Industrial engineers, corporate executives, research scientists, vice-presidents of advertising agencies—others of this stripe were joining the movement toward country and community. They shared a dissatisfaction with jobs repeatedly described as "meaningless," "abstract," and "boring"; and a thwarted yearning to return to a simpler rural existence. They could no longer tolerate commuting, the inflexibility of nine-to-five schedules, and the deteriorating quality and increasing cost of urban life.[18]

Is such a yearning for a simpler rural life an atavistic regression? It certainly is if the ex-urbanite fails to recognize that nature also imposes her discipline and her rigid time schedules. But if the new homesteader can accept this discipline, learn to work and plan with nature, he can help to work out a viable alternative to the prevailing techno-culture and its insane policy of infinite progress and growth on a finite planet.

Such alternatives are vitally important at this time, and the position which informs this essay is that any alternative is an alternative to some form of totalitarianism, however benign it may appear at this point. Theodore Roszak, along with other cultural critics such as Gibson Winter, Charles Reich, Paul Goodman, and Herbert Marcuse, has sought to unmask the subliminal aspects of technocratic control. "So subtle and so well rationalized have the arts of technocratic domination become in our advanced industrial societies that even those in the state and/or corporate structure who dominate our lives must find it impossible to conceive of themselves as the agents of a totalitarian control," writes Roszak.[19] The mass production of goods requires mass-man for their consumption, but this is an unhealthy situation. Ecologists warn that as an ecosystem is simplified it becomes increasingly unstable. The diversified mini-farm of the homesteader is an alternative to the monoculture which characterizes so much of commercial agriculture. And just as the durability of the ecosystem depends on diversity, so our social, economic, and political institutions could be strengthened by the "new" elements which the revolution in youth culture has introduced as alternatives to the prevailing techno-culture. The new homesteading movement provides alternatives to urban life and its sense of dispossession and meaningless labor, to the "need" to consume artificial goods and inferior products, to the ideology of progress and futurism, and to an economy based on the idea of scarcity. Let us examine these issues in greater detail.

The readers' letters in periodicals such as *Countryside* or *The Mother Earth News* make it perfectly obvious that the factors which push people back to the country are the over-crowding, the sense of rootlessness, the tensions and the deteriorating quality of city life. These "earth people" naturally want a place of their own in the country. Robert Ardrey suggests that this desire for land may be our genetic inheritance and thus more natural than we usually think.

> As our populations expand, as a world-wide movement from countryside to city embraces all peoples, as problems of housing, of broken homes and juvenile delinquency, of mass education and delayed independence of the young rise about us in our every human midst, as David Riesman's phrase "the lonely crowd" comes more and more aptly to describe all human-kind, have we not the right to ask: Is what we are witnessing, in essence, not the first consequence of the deterritorializing of man? And if man is a territorial animal, then as we seek to repair his dignity and responsibility as a human being, should we not first search for a means of restoring his dignity and responsibility as a proprietor?[20]

The Homestead Act of 1862 was an attempt to provide ownership of land with little or no cash investment, and thousands of family farms began in that way. Since then we have witnessed the decline of this family farm until today less than ten percent of the people in this country are farmers. And, of course, there are very few land-owners in our large cities.

In view of the fact that so few people in the inner city have real property (and the dignity and security of ownership that goes with it), an "Urban Homestead Act" has been proposed for America's cities.[21] It is a sensible proposal and it deserves support. People will continue to live in cities, and urban life must be humanized. But, given the absurd concentration of people in cities already, one must ask whether it would not be possible also to help in the resettlement of those who already want to move back to the land —especially at a time when increasing automation and/or economic recession threaten to create even greater unemployment. The fact that there are people who actually want to go back to the land should not be overlooked, for, as Ralph Borsodi pointed out, "history records almost no instance in which landless city dwellers abandoned city life until they were driven into the country by famine, pestilence or warfare."[22] Already in 1962 Russell Lord perceived a movement "outward from the jammed-up rim of suburbia toward modest country places and a certain amount of small-scale farming," and he argues that it could easily be given Federal support and encouragement. "If subsidies, inducement payments, and the mechanisms of government and private credit can serve, as they have in the main, to crowd families out of farming, changed laws and agencies with the power of the government behind them could surely stem such a trend and reverse it toward any designed measure of a more sensible and healthful farm and nonfarm ratio."[23] If the notion of homesteading—the farm as home, the home as a productive unit—comes into vogue, even in Washington, a new era in sane and healthy living could result.

Private philanthropic efforts are being made to help small farmers remain on the land, especially in the South. The Rural Advancement Fund of the National Sharecropper's Fund, for example, aims to counteract discriminatory national agricultural policies by helping black farmers develop cooperative and organic farming methods so that they can live on the land with health and dignity. Such efforts should also be the concern of the Department of Agriculture, and they should be given priority over efforts to increase production.

But American Agribusiness, as promoted by the Department of Agriculture, is a division of the Corporate Technocratic State, and it is so production-oriented that it seems capable only of bigness and growth. According to Mr. Lord, who had spent a lifetime in agricultural administration,

> commercial farm interests and the cold-blooded school of economic statisticians alike are forever asserting that 90 percent of the American farm output comes from the "top" 50 percent of our farms, with the other

percent producing a paltry dab of the total output. These efficiency experts, lay and professional, flinch at the very thought of such piddling producers and cry it forth that so many "little" operators working "inadequate" holdings, part time or full time, will surely reduce both unit and total crop yields and levels of productive efficiency.[24]

The question of efficiency is not just a matter of yield and production. It is obvious, given the embarrassing surpluses we already have, that we do not need a quantitative increase, but we do need ways to increase the production of healthy, quality food. Whether the methds of large-scale chemical farming produce better food is questionable. Moreover, increased bigness may actually curtail productivity. Robert Ardrey points out that "private plots occupy about 3 percent of all Russian cultivated land, yet they produce almost half of all vegetables consumed, almost half of all milk and meat, three-quarters of all eggs, and two-thirds of that staff of Russian life, potatoes."[25] This may prove something about private (not corporation) enterprise, to be sure, but Ardrey does also point out that the factory farm in Russia was simply inefficient in contrast to carefully tended small plots. Finally, statistics on production do not consider the fact that the farm homestead is not merely a production unit but a home, and this is the important thing about it.

The technological revolution in agriculture and food processing, ranging from chemically-stimulated growth to additives and preservatives, has kept pace with an unhealthy tendency in American life generally. As Alan Watts summed it up, "we are living in a culture which has been hypnotized with symbols—words, numbers, measures, quantities, and images—and . . . we mistake them for, and prefer them to, physical reality."[26] Or, as Charles Reich put it, "the Corporate State draws its vitality by a procedure that impoverishes the natural world. It grows by a process we shall call 'impoverishment by substitution.' "[27] He who complains about this strange kind of "growth" is asked, "And what would you put in its place?" The new homesteader has an answer: "The natural thing." His alternative to eating processed or "plastic" food is to raise his own food and bake his own bread. The recent concern over the deleterious effects of some chemical additives in "store-bought" food indicates that the desire for organic food is not just the faddish quirk of a few quacks. Indeed, homesteaders here, as in Russia, are finding that they can sell their surplus organically-grown food at a premium and thus earn the cash they need.

Productive and self-sufficient homesteads in the countryside would serve the need for environmental improvement better than the suburban sprawl which now surrounds our cities. During the depression of the 1930's a project such as this was begun near Dayton, Ohio with the support of the Subsistence Homestead Division under the Secretary of the Interior—then Harold L. Ickes. The project did not succeed, according to Ralph Borsodi, who served as a consulting economist for it and helped to plan it, because "the palsied hand of bureaucracy has been laid upon it."[28] Perhaps the homesteading movement of today, which has emerged by choice rather than out of economic necessity, and independently of governmental support, stands a better chance of success.

The homesteading movement which is emerging out of the cultural revolution of the past decade is an alternative to the still dominant ideology of progress, with its future orientation. Philip Slater comments on this difference between the old and the new culture.

> The hippie movement, for example, is brimming with nostalgia—a nostalgia peculiarly American and shared by old-culture adherents. This nostalgia embraces the Old West, Amerindian culture, the wilderness, the simple life, the utopian community—all venerable American traditions. But for the old culture they represent a subordinate, ancillary aspect of the culture, appropriate for recreational occasions or fantasy representations—a kind of pastoral relief from everyday striving—whereas for the new culture they are dominant themes. The new culture's passion for memorabilia, paradoxically, causes uneasiness in old-culture adherents, whose future-oriented invidiousness leads to a desire to sever themselves from the past.[29]

There are surely many reasons why Americans have felt that they can move into the future only by severing themselves from the past (the immigrant's attempt to become Americanized, for example), but this tendency has so impoverished the quality and richness of our lives that we have begun to suffer the disease Alvin Toffler has called "future shock." And Toffler, even as he notices that the new culture in America is trying to ease the strains of future shock, is too infected with futurism himself to recognize the intrinsic value and significance of the new culture.

> Most of today's "intentional communities" or utopian colonies . . . reveal a powerful preference for the past. These may be of value to the individuals in them, but the society as a whole would be better served by utopian experiments based on super- rather than pre-industrial forms. In-

stead of a communal farm, why not a computer software company whose program writers live and work communally?[30]

One answer could be that only the farm offers the possibility of meaningful physical work. It is important to notice, moreover, that communes seek utopia in the past rather than in the future, reversing a trend which began with the Industrial Revolution, when Western man began to look to the future for that which the present denied him. The fact that young people are now looking backward does not mean that they are trying to go back in time—on the contrary, the tactic of looking backward probably represents the wave of the future. But the recognition that time goes on does not entail the attempt to deliberately sever oneself from the past; indeed, it is this repudiation of the past that causes future shock, not the oncoming future. The communards and homesteaders are trying, as Philip Slater said, "to built a future that does not always look to the future."[31] It is not only possible but desirable that the future should be enriched with things of value and ways of life kept from the past. And if it is necessary to go "back" to nature to establish our relationship to it, let us by all means go "back." What use is our awareness of history if it does not free us from the tyranny of historical determinism or from continual and impoverishing change? And what good is affluence if it means that nothing can be treasured?

The true meaning of affluence, as Philip Slater so lucidly points out, is that one is freed from competetive striving and from the compulsion to invest oneself in possessions. The old culture's compulsion to buy and to compete rested on the assumption of scarcity. But the new culture, says Slater, "is founded on a rejection of scarcity assumptions."[32] This is obviously a psychological process and not just a matter of economics. There would hardly be an actual abundance of goods if they were properly distributed, at least not as long as many of them are wasted on war, but there are enough if we do not grasp and hoard. If we live with the confidence that there is plenty (a feeling that comes naturally to the organic gardener), we no longer need to accumulate more things. We thus recognize that growth for the sake of growth is, as they say, the ideology of the cancer cell. It may even be that the voluntary poverty of the subsistence homesteader would very likely not have emerged except in a society that has experienced a glut of consumer goods. This has created misunderstandings which will never be wholly resolved as long as artificially created scarcity is so real for so many Americans, for it is inevitable that the homesteader should be resented by the Black or by the Chicano, who very seldom in their history could experience the land as a benign and hospitable reality. The land is psychically available to young people of middle class background, and perhaps economically feasible for them too, as it is not available to the "other" Americans. Perhaps this "class conflict" will subside if it is recognized that some people are deprived of material goods while others are deprived of meaningful work. If the middle-class homesteader shows that he is sincerely dedicated to voluntary poverty and really serious about living and working on the land others may come to understand his motives. It has happened that when "hip" communards in the country have worked hard they have won the respect and even friendship of their sceptical old-culture rural neighbors.

When all is said and done it must be acknowledged that the movement back to the land is a trickle compared to the flood of those leaving the farm. Perhaps numbers are not important, since enough are going back to show that it is a real possibility. Close to a hundred thousand farms continue to be abandoned in the United States each year as the small farmers are being crowded out. The new homesteading movement will not reclaim all these farms; indeed, they are not even available except in areas of marginal agricultural potential where a large-scale operation is not profitable. And perhaps the most marginal land should be preserved as wilderness areas. But the new homesteading movement is a state of mind as well as a topographical reality. The movement has, after all, taken only the first step into eutopia; the other foot is still in utopia, and its state of mind is similarly divided. Although it is confused, some characteristics of this state of mind in more general terms can be ventured here, and in thus moving on to a more abstract level we shall also gain the perspective necessary to make a critique of the movement.

Nothing is more important, in the long run, than the values and ideals which serve as the ultimate sanctions of a culture. Since utopian thought is a very sensitive barometer of the pressures that create change, an examination of utopian theory and practice can help us ascertain the direction of current cultural trends.

We noticed earlier that utopian thought since the Industrial Revolution has been futuristic and technological, a tradition which is carried on today by thinkers like Buckminster Fuller. But it is important also to notice that the creative wellsprings of this type of utopian thought have dried up, at least as far as the literary imagination is concerned. Chad Walsh almost belabors the obvious in his book *From Utopia to Nightmare* as he shows how contemporary "utopian" novels tend to be "dystopian." The Christianity of the major denominations in America, which has sanctioned this futuristic religion of progress, has also become secularized in the process. Although some religious thinkers defend the idea of a secular Christianity, in the perspective of the history of religions it can be seen as a fossilization. Thus it is not surprising that an older tradition of utopian thought has come back into currency. The shift from city to country and from future to past which we have discerned in the new homesteading movement can be seen as an expression of this older mythic strand in our utopian tradition. Northrop Frye has succinctly described these two archetypal structures.

> In Christianity the city is the form of the myth of *telos*, the New Jerusalem that is the end of the human pilgrimage. But there is no city in the Christian, or Judaeo-Christian, myth of origin: that has only a garden, and the two progenitors of what was clearly intended to be a simple and patriarchal society. In the story which follows, the story of Cain and Abel, Abel is the shepherd and Cain a farmer whose descendants build cities and develop the arts. The murder of Abel appears to symbolize the blotting out of an idealized pastoral society by a more complex civilization. In Classical mythology the original society appears as the Golden Age, to which we have referred more than once, again a peaceful and primitive society without the complications of later ones. In both our main literary traditions, therefore, the tendency to see the ideal society in terms of a lost simple paradise has a ready origin.[33]

The utopian refuses to believe that paradise is really, irrecoverably lost. And the American experience, with its emphasis on beginning again, which R.W.B. Lewis has emphasized in his book *The American Adam*, has reinforced this strand in our mythic heritage. The idea of recovering paradise and making a new start is important here because it provides an archetype for the homesteader's movement to eutopia. Let us consider this movement, then, in relation to the notion of returning to origins and a new beginning. And since there can be no new beginning unless there has been an end, let us consider the ways in which the new homesteading movement is an end as well as a beginning.

One goes "back" to nature, or "back" to the country, mythically speaking, because one is returning to paradise, to the place of origin. Many urban Americans, incidentally, still have parents or grandparents on the farm, and the return to the country is for them infused with memories of childhood and personal origins. The return to origins in a temporal sense is expressed by the primitivism, the voluntary poverty, and the anti-technological bias which characterizes so many rural communes. A relaxation of sexual mores can similarly be seen as an attempt to return to a non-repressive style of life. A commune called "Greenfeel" was an example of the attempt to regain a polymorphous sexuality. In his brief discussion of its demise Ron Norman explained that "a major part of Greenfeel was sexuality—we would run naked in the woods, feel our bodies alive all day, sleep together at night, have sex anytime: men and women and kids, without feeling perverted and guilty. We would be a primitive animal tribe."[34] Here the paradisiacal aspects of the return to nature are strongly expressed. And since the commune is a less repressive kind of society, this return makes possible a reappropriation of the human body.

If the rural communards and homesteaders express a nostalgia for paradise, for a new beginning, we must go on to ask what has ended. In pursuing this question it is possible to sense the powerful religious seriousness which motivates the movement. It is an eschatological phenomenon. Several aspects of the rural commune, aspects which seem to emerge spontaneously, conform rather closely to the morphology of various millenary movements or cargo cults. In his essay on "Cosmic and Eschatological Renewal," Mircea Eliade suggests that the "eschatological nudism" and sexual freedom which characterizes several such cults is the ritual anticipation of paradise.

> What Tsek [the cult founder] announces in his message is in fact the imminent restoration of Paradise on Earth. Men will no longer work; they will have no more need for tools, domestic animals or possessions. Once the old order is abolished the laws, rules, taboos will lose their reason. The prohibitions and customs sanctioned by tradition will give place to absolute liberty; in the first place to sexual liberty, to orgy. For, in human society, it is sexual life that is subject to the strictest taboos and constraints. To be free from laws, prohibitions and customs, is to rediscover primordial liberty and blessedness, the state which preceded the present human condition, in fact the paradisiacal state.[35]

Attitudes such as this are expressed by many contemporary communards, and their revolutionary thrust is obvious. The influence of neo-Freudian thought (Norman Brown and Wilhelm Reich, for example), the rediscovery of the body via LSD, various experiments in group marriage and pan-sexuality, Tantric non-orgasmic sexuality, all witness to the powerful desire to move beyond a repressive reality to the polymorphous sexuality of childhood and to the innocence of Adam before the Fall. Most communards have given up private possessions and hold all things in common. Thus Lou Gottlieb deeded his farm in California to God and freed it for Morning Star, an open-land commune. The "cargo" theme in this complex of paradisiacal attitudes is expressed in the widely-held belief that since production in an advanced industrial society is largely automated, and since prosperity depends on production and consumption, there will be free food and goods without working. The theme of free food also finds expression in the recent vogue for books like *Stalking the Wild Asparagus* by Euell Gibbons and in the enthusiasm for edible wild plants. It may be that such ideas are typical only of the "lunatic fringe" in the commune movement, but a reading of *Modern Man in Search of Utopia* or most other issues of *The Modern Utopian*, the comprehensive inter-commune periodical, will show that these are the kinds of ideas that find frequent literary expression.

It cannot be denied that the eschatological bias so prevalent in the commune movement, and especially in the so-called "hip" communes, is based on actual experience. The "end of the world" is experienced personally by the drop-out. As a former suburbanite matron in a commune explained to Robert Houriet, "I learned that you have to be completely busted and lose everything before you can become new and whole again. Praise the Lord."[36] Or the notion of the "end of the world" can be expressed and experienced through the imagery of environmental pollution and ecological catastrophe, racial strife, war and the demonic technocratic system that supports it—for a man-made system that has become autonomous and self-perpetuating is demonic. It is typical of a millenary movement that the old system is experienced as an evil and demonic reality that is about to collapse, while the "saving remnant" that has withdrawn from the system ritually anticipates, through drugs and music and dance, the paradise that will come after the old order has passed away.

The "hip" commune, then, probably expresses the most complete version of utopia as a regained paradise that has emerged in the West for a long time. Its eschatological and messianic aspects remain to be explored, though it is very likely that someone is hard at work right now on a study of "the Commune Movement as a Cargo Cult" or something like that.* The myth of a lost paradise, and nostalgia for it, is also quite naturally, though to a lesser degree, a part of the new homesteading movement as well. The eutopian is not yet free from utopian dreams and visions, nor should he be. But these utopian elements must be clearly recognized for what they are, and cherished as such, while the more practical business of establishing eutopia is going on. Nearly every group or cult that has been swept away by the full mythic power of its eschatological vision has also been led to disillusionment and destruction. It could happen again, though it is less likely to happen as the commune matures into a community.

One thing is certain: the pressures that generate a nostalgia for paradise and its peculiar eschatological orientation are real enough. The vitality of the old culture, urban technological civilization, is waning; it tries to maintain itself by force, dealing death instead of promoting life. The movement back to the land is a symptom of this social and political degradation and an alternative to it. "It should not suprise us," wrote Lewis Mumford, "if the foundations of eutopia were established in ruined countries; that is, in countries where metropolitan civilization has collapsed and where all its paper prestige is no longer accepted at its paper value." But the end of the old culture does not automatically generate the emergence of the new, and therefore, as Mumford went on to say, "the chief business of eutopians was summed up by Voltaire in the final injunction of Candide: Let us cultivate our garden."[37] God may have planted the first garden of Eden for man, but man has to plant and tend all others by himself.

In summary, then, we have seen that the movement from utopia to eutopia is a movement through *two* types of utopia. The first is the futuristic utopia of urban techno-culture where one tries to be at home in the world by finding one's "place" in the socio-economic system. The second is the paradisiacal utopia exemplified by the "hip" commune with its extravagant expectation of

---

*Whether these "hip" communes do indeed reflect the pervasive eschatological consciousness of the typical cargo cult or whether they merely herald the beginning of a new religion or a revitalization movement, analagous to the new religions in Japan, for example, will have to be discussed by a scholar who is more competent than I am. H. Byron Earhart has been seeking to clarify the methodological issues involved in this kind of problem relative to the new religions of Japan. See, for example, "The Interpretation of the 'New Religions' of Japan as Historical Phenomena," *Journal of the American Academy of Religion*, XXXVII (September, 1969), 237-248.

eschatological renewal. Although these utopians are drawn back to nature in their search for the lost paradise, they are uneasy about space, move about frantically, and dread the thought of being stuck in one place. The paradise they seek exists only in some mythical topography or in "middle earth." The new homesteader has moved beyond these utopias, for he remembers that the Earthly Paradise has already been found and needs only to be reappropriated. As Mircea Eliade explained in his essay on the mythical geography of paradise and utopia, the discovery and exploration of America was heavily freighted with the imagery of paradise—a New Beginning in a New World. Eliade goes on to point out that "the long resistance of American élites to the industrialization of the country, and their exaltation of the virtues of agriculture, may be explained by the same nostalgia for the Earthly Paradise."[38] Thus the mythic basis of essays such as the one I am now concluding is exposed! And given the fact that industrialization has triumphed, so that the earth and its resources are regarded as "raw materials" for the production of manufactured "goods," the resurgence of the myth of the Earthly Paradise may seem anachronistic. But the new homesteader has gone through every step of the modern experience; only after that did he rediscover the land and his place on it. As he becomes integrated with his physical environment and realizes his symbiotic relationship to the earth he encounters a reality which he recognizes as more primordial and more ultimate than the socio-economic system. It may even come to pass that the new homesteading movement will be seen as the beginning of a new or revitalized religious phenomenon which once again makes it possible to experience a sense of cosmic sacrality.

NOTES

1. Bill Kaysing, *First-Time Farmer's Guide* (San Francisco: Straight Arrow Books, 1971). This book contains a comprehensive and up-to-date bibliography of useful publications on the theory and practice of homesteading, pp. 297-310.
2. See Helen and Scott Nearing, *Living the Good Life* (Harborside, Maine: Social Sciences Institute, 1954, reprinted by Schocken Books in 1971), and Ralph Borsodi, *Flight from the City* (New York, 1933).
3. Ralph Borsodi, *This Ugly Civilization* (New York, 1929), p. 272. Borsodi's thought continues to be influential with the communal group at Heathcote 'Center where the School of Living publishes *The Green Revolution*.
4. Gibson Winter, *Being Free* (New York, 1970), p. 91.

5. Ibid., p. 105.
6. Charles Reich, *The Greening of America* (New York, 1970), p. 259.
7. Richard Underwood, "Ecological and Psychedelic Approaches to Theology," *Soundings*, 53 (Winter, 1969), p. 385.
8. Reich, p. 218.
9. Northrop Frye, "Varieties of Literary Utopias," in *Utopias and Utopian Thought*, ed. Frank E. Manuel (Boston, 1967), p. 28.
10. Robert Houriet, *Getting Back Together* (New York, 1971), p. 210.
11. Ibid., p. 215.
12. Ibid., p. 220.
13. John H. Todd, "Designing a New Science," *Organic Gardening and Farming* (October, 1971), 83-84.
14. Ibid., 83.
15. Aldo Leopold, "The Land Ethic," in *A Sand County Almanac* (New York, 1970), pp. 258-259.
16. Kurt Vonnegut, Jr., *Player Piano* (New York, 1970), p. 144.
17. Ibid., p. 147.
18. Houriet, *Getting Back Together*, p. 236.
19. Theodore Roszak, *The Making of a Counter Culture* (Garden City, New York, 1969), p. 9.
20. Robert Ardrey, *The Territorial Imperative* (New York, 1971), pp. 94-95.
21. James H. Davis, "The Urban Homestead Act," *Landscape*, 19 (Winter, 1970 [published July, 1971]), pp. 11-23.
22. Borsodi, *This Ugly Civilization*, p. 316.
23. Russell Lord, *The Care of the Earth* (New York, 1963), p. 344.
24. Ibid., p. 345.
25. Ardrey, *The Territorial Imperative*, p. 107.
26. Alan Watts, *Does it Matter?* (New York, 1971), pp. 36-37.
27. Reich, *The Greening of America*, p. 158.
28. Borsodi, *Flight from the City*, p. xviii. A description of this homesteading project is included as a postlude to the book, pp. 151-171. Russell Lord implied (in *The Care of the Earth*, pp. 280-281) that the project was aborted because it was thought to be communistic.
29. Philip Slater, *The Pursuit of Loneliness* (Boston, 1971), p. 109.
30. Alvin Toffler, *Future Shock* (New York, 1970), p. 414. Toffler's book reads like a book on pornography: while ostensibly showing the dangers of rapid social change, he appears to derive a perverse kind of enjoyment from presenting the data.
31. Slater, *The Pursuit of Loneliness*, p. 142.
32. Ibid., p. 139.
33. Frye, "Varieties of Literary Utopias," *op. cit.*, p. 40.
34. Ron Norman, "Greenfeel: Final Notes on an Intentional Community," *Alternatives Newsmagazine*, 1971, p. 17. This is a publication of Alternatives! Foundation, which also publishes *The Modern Utopian*.

35. Mircea Eliade, *The Two and the One* (New York, 1969), p. 127.
36. Houriet, *Getting Back Together*, p. 94.
37. Lewis Mumford, *The Story of Utopias* (New York, 1922), pp. 306-307.
38. Mircea Eliade, "Paradise and Utopia: Mythical Geography and Eschatology," in *Utopias and Utopian Thought*, ed. Manuel, p. 269.

COMMUNES AND THE RECONSTRUCTION
OF REALITY

JAY AND HEATHER OGILVY*

IF A DISTRAUGHT MOTHER asks her son or daughter, "Why, in God's name, are you joining this commune?" she might get the answer: "Oh, I dunno. I feel like it." Not much to go on. Mother would be more satisfied, though more appalled at the prospect of a wasted education, if son or daugher were an articulate, Ivy-League drop-out who replied: "Philip Slater says we need a new society stressing cooperation rather than competition, and Paul Goodman shows the need for community as a decentralized alternative to our inefficient, centralized mass society, and just about all the sociologists show that the nuclear family is a complete, mess, mother!"

The more articulate answer can be extended virtually without limit. As impressive as the conscious reasons for communal living

Heather and Jay Ogilvy have lived in a commune in New Haven since 1969. Mrs. Ogilvy has taught nursery school, worked with psychodrama, and is presently enrolled in a program at Yale in community mental health and public health education. Mr. Ogilvy is an assistant professor of philosophy at Yale, teaching classes in German idealism, nineteenth century continental philosophy, and a new course entitled "Community and Utopia."

*While we are solely responsible for the shapes given to the ideas in this article, many of the ideas were born from the ups and downs of a shared experience involving some eighteen adults and six children (though never more than fourteen adults and four children at one time) over the past two years. It is hard to adequately acknowledge their contributions, e.g. the whole idea of multiple reality constructions is contained in the Tom Wolfe/Ken Kesey metaphor of trying to get others into your own movie (*The Electric Kool-Aid Acid Test*), a metaphor which one of our number often used to make sense of our experience. But in order to protect the privacy of our friends we will neither be very specific about our own experiences, nor will we be more specific in our gratitude than to acknowledge our debt collectively.

may be, however, we propose to look instead at an important motivating feature of which son or daughter may be totally unaware: the need for a set of categories in terms of which a coherent reality can be constituted. Unless the prospective communard has assimilated the strange sounding truths of Kantian philosophy (and its legacy in the sociology of knowledge, of which more below), it is highly unlikely that the reasons for communal living will include the so-called transcendental argument.

Kant described as transcendental any features of consciousness which are necessary for a coherent experience to be possible. It is worth pausing on the concept of the transcendental because even today it is probably true that most people think of "experience," "reality," "objectivity," and related concepts in a manner that post-Kantian philosophers would call pre-Kantian. Reality, it is thought, is *given*. It is allegedly objective in the sense that its basic features are independent of subjective influence. Aberrations such as occasional color-blindness there may be, but for the most part the order of experience is the order given by objective reality.

As a corollary to the pre-Kantian view it will follow that if reality is experienced as incoherent and disordered it is assumed to be reality's fault. If experience goes haywire we look for objective causes: the decline of the Judeo-Christian tradition, mass society, technology, future shock, etc. The pre-Kantian may then conclude that experience has gone haywire because it is the experience of a single, given reality that has gone haywire: history run amok.

Without denying a certain truth to much of what the pre-Kantian says, we would like to stress the other side of what must finally be viewed, with Hegel,* as a dialectical relation between history and constitutive consciousness as the determinants of experience. We wish to stress, at least temporarily, the role played by the categories brought into play by an individual consciousness in its attempt to constitute its experience of reality. In stressing the

---

*While granting the importance of Kant's contribution of the transcendental perspective, Hegel and the subsequent historicist tradition recognized the capacity for change exhibited by constitutive categories. Some categories or other are necessary for experience to be possible, but not everyone need share the same constellation of categories for everyone to have some experience or other. Hegel and Nietzsche stressed the importance of different times generating different realities, anthropologists showed the effect of differing cultures in different places, and finally Karl Mannheim established the sociology of knowledge as concerned primarily with the perspectives of different classes at one time and place.

transcendental approach we hardly intend a Kantian epistemology of the commune movement, perish the thought. We simply wish to distinguish our approach from any analysis which seeks to determine the direct and immediate influences of social patterns on communal experience, or vice versa. Instead we ask about the indirect and mediated influence; how social patterns influence the subjective cetegorial scheme which in turn influences the experience of reality—quite a different question than how social patterns directly influence the reality experienced.

Returning, then, to the inarticulate offspring who doesn't know why he wants to join a commune, let's suppose for a moment that his is the most honest response: there is no definitive reason for his choice. But that in itself is precisely the reason for his choice. Let us spell out this paradoxical formulation.

Sometimes people do things for reasons which others can understand. Johnny goes to Harvard because he thinks he can get a good education there, and education is important to personal growth and fulfillment, as well as to material gain, social status, increasing one's capacity to help others, etc. Johnny's admission to Harvard will be an occasion for universal joy to him and his family, not just because they all want Johnny to go to Harvard for the reasons just given, but also because for once they all want the same thing—whatever it is. They not only choose the same thing; they also understand one another's choices. This is important, for the capacity to make non-arbitrary choices depends on having reasons for choosing, and it is easier to be confident in your reasons for choosing when those around you share the same reasons.*

If people cease to share the same determinants of choice (we hesitate to use the term "values" because values are only one part of a comprehensive categorial scheme), then they find it more difficult to understand one another's choices. As a result one not only fails to see the sense behind the actions of others (history run amok), but further, one fails to get the reinforcement for the constellation of categories, reasons, and values with which one is valiantly though privately trying to make sense of one's own ex-

*For a classic study representing the considerable literature on the importance of positive reinforcement for individual judgment, see Morton Deutsch and Harold Gerard, "A Study of Normative and Informational Social Influences upon Individual Judgment," *Journal of Abnormal and Social Psychology*, 51 (1955), 629-636.

perience. So when son says he doesn't know why he wants to join the commune it is not that he knows but cannot communicate his knowledge across the yawning generation gap; it may be that he genuinely does not know. It may be that he is not in possession of a categorial scheme that would permit the coherent formulation of reasons. And that is why he wants to join the commune: to provide the conditions of mutual reinforcement for the shoring up of a shattered categorial scheme. He cannot articulate this reason for his choice, *even to himself*; and that is precisely the reason for his choice.

The need for some sort of experiential ordering is hardly peculiar to today's youth. It is just that the rest of society has satisfied this need in different ways, ways which for various reasons are often repugnant to prospective communards, e.g. marriage. The role of marriage and the family as a context for reinforcing categorial schemes has been excellently portrayed by Peter Berger and Hansfried Kellner. In an article entitled "Marriage and the Construction of Reality,"[1] to which the present paper owes more than just its title, Berger and Kellner argue that a sense of reality is "sustained through conversation with significant others" (53), and that "marriage occupies a privileged status among the significant validating relationships for adults in our society" (53). Much of what they have to say about marriage holds true without change for communes, and that which is true only of marriage suggests by contrast other enlightening truths about communes.

Berger and Kellner show both the need for the family as a context for reinforcing patterns of reality structuring, and the difficulties involved in successfully achieving reinforcement rather than conflict:

> As of the marriage, most of each partner's actions must now be projected in conjunction with those of the other. Each partner's definitions of reality must be continually correlated with the definitions of the other. The other is present in nearly all horizons of everyday conduct. Furthermore the identity of each now takes on a new character, having to be constantly matched with that of the other, indeed being typically perceived by people at large as being symbiotically conjoined with the identity of the other. In each partner's psychological economy of significant others, the marriage partner becomes the other *par excellence*, the nearest and most decisive coinhabitant of the world. Indeed all other significant relationships have to be almost automatically reperceived and regrouped in accordance with this drastic shift. (58)

Two questions arise: first, to what extent does communal life require a similar "drastic shift" involving significant others and a reperception of outside acquaintances? and second, to the extent that both a marriage and a commune serve the same functions for their members, what kind of context does a commune provide for a marriage? Will the two complement one another, the one making up for the weaknesses of the other, or will the demands of significance compete with one another? This is not the old question of jealousy, but a rather more subtle question of determining the complex relationship between institutions which are themselves complex, and the effects those complexities will have on the persons involved. Let us take the first question first, since its answer will bear on the answer to the second.

To what extent, then, does communal life require the kind of "drastic shift" involved in getting married? First of all, there are communes and communes. While all marriages in our society share at least the common features of a legal bond to one other person, communes vary tremendously with respect to the number of people involved, the type of commitment expected, the degree of spatial and cultural separation from "straight society," etc. The best we can do, then, is point out certain syndromes of interpersonal dynamics while admitting that the intensity and significance of these syndromes will depend on the different variables mentioned.

Put most simply, we shall argue that communes do require a similar "drastic shift" in one's world, and that, depending on the type of commune, the shift is either easier or harder to make than in marriage. The inevitability of the need for a drastic shift is worth emphasizing because, as with marriage, it is precisely this shift which is liable to be unanticipated and therefore shocking and unsettling. Speaking of the shift demanded by a marriage, Berger and Kellner write: "Now, the full implications of this fact are rarely apprehended by the protagonists with any degree of clarity. There rather is to be found the notion that one's world, one's other-relationships and, above all, oneself have remained what they were before—only, of course, that world, others, and self will now be shared with the marriage partner. It should be clear by now that this notion is a grave misapprehension" (58-59). This strikes us as an accurate description of the expectations and experiences of many of those who join communes. Of course there are those who join specialized and sometimes highly religious communes with the express intention of gaining enlightenment and total transformation; but speaking of those who are primarily seeking a network of relationships with others like themselves, and not of those seeking a master, the point holds that the demands of those relationships are liable to be misapprehended.

In talks we had before moving into a commune we recall several times when the point was raised: "What about outside connections? Is the expectation that the commune should monopolize our whole social life?" Since we were not planning the rural agrarian trip, but had among our number several graduate students and professional people, we unanimously willed to maintain all of our outside contacts and share them with others in the commune. Ideally we hoped to have space for a guest room, and we would certainly welcome guests for dinner. Yet the hopes were hard to maintain.

Berger and Kellner use the example of a male partner's relationships with male friends before and after a marriage. "It is a common observation that such relationships, especially if the extramarital partners are single, rarely survive the marriage, or, if they do, are drastically redefined after it" (59). The point is not that the wife is jealous, or that her dislike of her husband's friends leads her to undermine the previous friendship. "What rather happens, very simply, is a slow process in which the husband's image of his friend is transformed as he keeps talking about his friend with his wife. Even if no actual talking goes on, the mere presence of the wife forces him to see his friend differently" (59).

In a commune situation, either a similar process takes place, or, if commune members maintain "significant ongoing conversation" with people outside the commune, it is difficult to avoid using those relationships to reinforce and solidify whatever negative feelings they may be experiencing toward others within the commune—just as the husband, in the previous illustration, might react from the drastic shift marriage demands by talking more about his wife with his friend than about his friend with his wife. Needless to say, both the marriage relationship and the relationships with others in the commune are liable to suffer from outside contacts serving such a function. Again, this threat to the marriage or commune need have nothing to do with evil intentions or unfriendliness, any more than the fading of a friendship between husband and buddy follows from intentional sabotage by the wife. This inexorable dynamic follows from banal facts of human economy: how many hours one can spend in close proximity with selected persons. Precisely the banality of this dynamic tends to obscure its importance in the eyes of anyone faced with the romance of conjugal love or communal brotherhood. But after all, the thing that distinguishes a network of close friendships from a commune most obviously is the fact of living together spending many hours in close proximity with selected persons.

While it may be easier to maintain old friendships after joining a commune than after getting married, it is probably more difficult, or at least less likely, for one to enter new friendships after joining a commune than after getting married. Being only two, married partners naturally seek out new friends to enrich their social and emotional life. Furthermore, being only two, they can easily do so together. In a commune on the other hand the sheer number of "significant others" provides a perhaps overrich social and emotional life. And if one does try to widen the circle by bringing in a new friend, unanimous acceptance is far more difficult to attain with twelve than two. If a single person feels ill at ease bringing a prospective mate home to meet the parents, imagine the possibilities for tension bringing a prospective mate home to meet the commune.

The issue of unanimity arises in more contexts than the choice of friends. What color shall we paint the house? How shall we arrange who cooks when? How do we want to furnish the house? These and many other seemingly trivial questions elicit answers which in their variety provike the more serious questions: How are we to arrive at decisions? Does everybody have to be in on every decision, or do we prefer anarchy? Though discussions before moving into a commune may reflect no fixed, or strongly held ideologies, the series of day-to-day small questions will invariably bring out in each person a constellation of the ways he prefers to structure his world. None of the particular decisions seems worth the effort of a disagreement; people of good will can be flexible on particular points. But more than good will is required to remold an entire constellation of reality determinants. This is true of marriage as well, but in a commune unanimity is harder to attain. Even granting the possibility of a hard-won compromise between John and Jane—the kind of compromise they could work out if they were married to one another—Jane's drastic shift toward John may be a shift away from Jean. "Away" and "toward" have nothing to do with affection in this context. Closeness here means similarity in the ways two people structure reality. Difficulty in achieving this kind of closeness increases drastically with an increase in the number of reality structurers involved. Even granting a willingness to move from "where one is at," each person faces a vastly complicated problem. To use a geometric metaphor, whereas a straight line marks a clear and simple path as the shortest distance between two points, finding the point which marks the easiest "compromise" in an array of eight or ten points presents more difficulties.

But surely, it will be said, everyone does not have to be "in the same place" all the time. This sounds like some sort of group totalitarianism. Isn't the real solution to share only a respect and appreciation for differences, a healthy pluralism?

Here we arrive at an important parting of the ways, a difference that distinguishes one type of commune from another and often distinguishes members of a single commune into two separate camps. Let us call those on the one side the monists and those on the other the pluralists.* The monists want to find the center which identifies the shared core of the commune, whatever that shared core may be. The pluralists see a rich communal life in terms of all "doing their own thing." Their tolerance and pluralism may even extend to the point of telling the monists that its fine for monists to do their monistic thing. But of course that answer cannot satisfy the monistic demand for having not just the monists but all the rest locating themselves around the common core. The use of labels naturally makes this split sound more clear-cut than it is ever likely to be in fact; there are those in the middle, and in two years' experience we felt ourselves move from one persuasion to the other. But clear or obscure the distinction is felt in many communes with which we've been acquainted.

Speaking of the same distinction as one between communes rather than within them, let us now compare the two different types of communes, first with respect to the degree of difficulty involved in reaching unanimity, and second with respect to marriage as a private context for the construction of reality. The separate comparisons are quite obvious, but together they constitute an interesting commentary on the differences between

---

*Though we are responsible for the following elaboration of the monist/pluralist distinction, we are indebted to Jon Roush of The Learning Community in Portland, Oregon for our first hearing of the distinction so perspicuously named and described.

marriage and commune, and second, on the viability of the pluralists' seemingly plausible answer to the demand for unanimity.

Religiously or politically oriented communes, or those centered around a charismatic leader, will be most clearly recognized as
monistic communes. The common core is the obvious *raison d'etre*
for the commune. Given a common ideology or a single, ultimate
decision maker, unanimity will be easy to reach, probably easier
than in marriages based on love. Monistic communes will then
function well as private contexts for the construction of reality.
Pluralistic communes, on the other hand, are liable to function less
well, since unanimity or compromise will be difficult to reach;
consequently it is worth asking whether pluralistic communes can
serve at all as contexts for reinforcing a member's mode of
structuring reality, or whether the pluralistic commune does not
tend to shatter rather than shore up one's own categorial scheme.
Precisely to the extent that it is private and therefore intimate,
the pluralistic commune may be a greater enemy than the public
world against one's efforts to fashion a coherent reality.

Fortunately the picture of the pluralistic commune need not
be as bleak as all this, though the danger is real. In order to
vindicate the pluralistic commune, however, it will be necessary
to question some of Berger and Kellner's central assumptions.
Their study projects a picture in which validation of one's reality
is a desperate process relying only on social support. We find
lacking in this picture an appreciation for the fact that constellations of reality determinants differ widely with respect to their
capacity for organically structuring a coherent reality. Berger and
Kellner seem to suggest that all incipient categorial schemes not
only need massive support but also can use that support to maintain a reality. We wish to suggest that some coherently projected
realities need relatively little support while other projected realities will issue only in a magnified incoherence and schizophrenic
unreality for all the apparent objectivity and fixity rendered by
social support.

The point is not that some prospective realities are bad and
others good to the extent that they correspond to Reality or
realize absolute values. Such an argument would beg the question
of social reality's artifactual character. The point is rather that not
just any grab-bag of categories and values is sufficient to determine
a reality, let alone Reality. Clearly some sort of conflict (rather
than complementarity) often pertains between different reality

determinants. Otherwise why would two people experience difficulty and pain in trying to correlate their pictures of reality? But what kind of conflict is it?

Part of our complaint with the Berger and Kellner study is that it nowhere offers a clear answer to this question. Consequently we can hardly criticize an "answer" quoted from their text. For them to reach the conclusions they do, however, it seems that they are presupposing a musical chairs type of conflict: after the honeymoon is over and the music stops there are only so many chairs and too many reality determinants. If two reality determinants end up sitting next to one another it has less to do with how they relate to one another than with the strength that propelled them into their seats.

But logical contradiction constitutes another model of conflict, one which takes seriously the structure of juxtaposed claimants. Whereas the musical chairs model stresses the relation between the many-termed whole and a prospective part, while remaining indifferent to the structure of dyadic relations between particular parts, logical contradiction stresses the dyadic relation at the expense of remaining indifferent to the whole being constituted by the parts. What is needed here is a more complex model according to which the lack of a "fit" between two terms follows neither from a "lack of room" for more than one term, nor from a logical contradiction stemming purely from the structure and contents of the two terms alone; a lack of fit will rather be a function of both the contents of the two terms and the way each separately and both together relate to the rest of the terms in the whole.

---

*As incomplete as the present model of conflict and coherence may be, its specifications are considerably more rigorous than some other accounts which are clearly striving after a model to do the same job. See, for example, Charles Reich's loose description of what he means by consciousness in his accounts of Consciousness I, Consciousness II and Consciousness III in *The Greening of America* (New York, 1970), pp. 14-15. Similarly, Berger and Luckmann gloss over the problem of the "logic" of non-logical conflict or cohesion when they treat the relationships between various processes of socialization and institutionalization: "In principle, institutionalization may take place in any area of collectively relevant conduct. In actual fact, sets of institutionalization processes take place concurrently. There is no *a priori* reason for assuming that these processes will necessarily 'hang together' functionally, let alone as a logically consistent system" (Berger and Luckmann, *The Social Construction of Reality*, p. 63). Our model is intended as a more precise description of what it is to "hang together" functionally.

The best guides to the development of such a model come from the organic world and from art. Life and beauty both mark just such a successful synthesis of related terms. Yet it is notoriously difficult to reduce both life and beauty to clearly definable, logical patterns. Let it suffice, then, that we have given the requirements for the model and a guide for its understanding, if not a detailed construction of the model itself.

Returning now from the harsh light of logical analysis to the shade of pluralistic communes, let us ask how our model of conflict and complementarity reflects on the quest for unanimity. Earlier we suggested the possibility that pluralistic communes might pose a threat rather than serve as an assistance to an individual's construction of reality. Now we are in a position to suggest conditions under which such a threat might be beneficial rather than destructive. Granted that the reality construction process is a social process both before and after joining a commune, if an individual joins a commune after having internalized reality determinants which do not form a coherent whole,* then life in a pluralistic commune can serve as a beneficial sorting-out process. Such a process can take place more easily in a pluralistic commune than in the limited and highly determinate confines of marriage or a monistic commune. Because alternatives are available (rather than the straight line between two points), there need be no sense of a desperate "make it or break it" construction with a fixed and limited set of tools and materials. Of course the danger exists that an individual with an incoherent set of reality determinants might refuse to acknowledge the need for a sorting out process. Then the availability of alternatives will still

---

*For a vivid account showing the radical incoherence of the directives to be internalized by a young person in our society, see Barry Stevens, "Curtain Raiser," in Carl Rogers and Barry Stevens, *Person to Person* (New York, 1971), pp. 1ff: "Sit nicely. Leave the room to blow your nose. Don't do that, that's silly. Why, the poor child doesn't even know how to pick a bone! Flush the toilet at night because if you don't it makes it harder to clean. Don't flush the toilet at night—you wake people up! Always be nice to people. Even if you don't like them, you mustn't hurt their feelings. Be frank and honest. If you don't tell people what you think of them, that's cowardly. Butter knives. It is important to use butter knives. Butter knives? What foolishness! Speak nicely. Sissy! Kipling is wonderful! Ugh! Kipling (turning away).

"The most important thing is to have a career. The most important thing is to get married. The hell with everyone. Be nice to everyone. The most important thing is sex. The most important thing is to have money in the bank . . . " And so on.

seem a threat rather than an opportunity. The shadow of danger is real, but marriage stands in the same shade.

But what about the lucky few who emerge from adolescence having managed to internalize a coherent set of categories? Would there be any point in their joining a pluralistic commune? From Berger and Kellner's point of view, certainly not. "Since ... the objectivation that constitutes this reality is precarious, the groups with which the couple associates are called upon to assist in code-fining the new reality. The couple is pushed toward groups that strengthen their new definition of themselves and the world, avoids those that weaken this definition" (60). They claim that the ongoing conversation in which their reality is "talked through" "has a very important result—namely, a hardening or stabilization of the common objectivated reality" (61).

Just as we find in their study a lack of any discrimination between more and less coherent constellations of reality deter-minants, so we find no suggestion of a rhythm of support and discriminating critique. But just as a healthy organism grows, sometimes going through significant metamorphoses, so even the most coherent reality might endure more vigorously if sustained by occasional challenge and change rather than by uninterrupted support for "stabilization," "hardening," even ossification. Berger and Kellner's description is no doubt true of most marriages, but we question their judgment of necessity for the process: "In the most far-reaching sense of the word, the married individual 'settles down'—and *must* do so, if the marriage is to be viable, in accor-dance with its contemporary institutional definition" (63). Even if we grant, for the sake of argument, their radical acceptance of contemporary society,* surely the contemporary institutional definition of marriage includes survival if not bliss, and we wonder whether growth and change are not in the long run better tools for survival in our contemporary society than uncritical support and stabilization.

Our critique of Berger and Kellner brings us back, not unin-tentionally, to a question posed some time ago: What about the

---

*Cf. p. 65: "The narrowing and stabilization of identity is functional in a society that, in its major public institutions, must insist on rigid controls over the individual's conduct. At the same time, the narrow enclave of the nuclear family serves as a macrosocially innocuous 'play area,' in which the individual can safely exercise his world-building proclivities without upsetting any of the important social, economic, and political apple carts."

commune as a context for marriage? We've just used marriage as an analogue for the lucky person who enters a commune with a coherent reality pattern utterly intact. What has he to gain from challenge? Growth, we answer, and the same holds for an at least temporarily happy and compatible marriage. But as few need to be reminded, not all marriages are happy or compatible. First, let us consider new marriages.

Though a young boy may laugh and play, Aristotle wisely remarks that "a boy is not happy, for he is not yet capable of such acts, owing to his age; and boys who are called happy are being congratulated by reason of the hopes we have for them."[2] Similarly, despite the blush of honeymoon bliss, a new marriage is not properly speaking "a happy marriage." The process of mutual discovery and creation has not yet taken place. Furthermore, from what we have seen a commune may not be the best environment in which to let this process take place. As our geometrical metaphor suggested, the stresses of marriage and commune will be pulling the individual marriage partners in different directions. If two people decide to get married in the first place, then they need a good deal of time and most of their energies to discover whether they can construct a single unit with a single reality, or whether they are and must remain two separate individuals supporting two different (even if rarely separate) realities.

If two people do find they constitute a pair with a shared reality, then they can enter a pluralistic commune as one. As the above analogy suggests, they might keep their happiness from being merely temporary. Precisely by avoiding stabilization and hardening they might prevent their happiness from turning into what Nietzsche called that wretched contentment of the twosome, and from thence into a hubristic pride before a middle-aged fall.

And what of the plight of the incompatible? Here we see the pluralistic commune as possibly playing a very beneficial role. If two people discover that they structure their realities in significantly different ways, they have, in a sense, created the minimal and most intense pluralistic commune. They are liable to threaten rather than support one another's realities, however much they may love one another. If each finds himself utterly without support for his or her reality, then we are inclined to agree with Berger in Kellner that anomie and unhappiness will be the result. The advantages of a pluralistic commune to an incompatible couple are several: first, each may find with other members of the commune support for his or her reality. This is obvious. Less obvious, but perhaps more important as far as the dynamics of the marriage are concerned, is the possibility that each will become less defensive and consequently less critical of the other's reality scheme. It is safe to respect the other when one's own reality is not under attack. When it is a daily experience to have one's reality under siege, however subtly, then it is proper to speak of what existential psychoanalysts call ontological insecurity. And for this the surest cure is a day-to-day buttressing of one's reality rather than a week-to-week visit to the existential psychoanalyst.

Even where it's not as bad as all that, the experience of support to offset the friction of an incompatible marriage can lessen the very friction that might have come to have seemed a given. At best two people might come to appreciate the differences that had earlier seemed so threatening. As Hegel noted, "spirit is all the greater the greater the opposition out of which it returns to itself,"[3] and more recently Jung has said, "The greater the contrast, the greater is the potential. Great energy only comes from a correspondingly great tension between opposites."[4] If the previous paragraphs on incompatible spouses' needs for support show our agreement with much of Berger and Kellner's study, our choice of these quotations shows the direction in which we feel their study needs to be supplemented.

Too often the communal support of one reality will mean only the expansion of "we precious two" to "we precious few." The pluralistic commune, on the other hand, is a living lesson in tolerance for its members, both with respect to one another and with respect to the "outside world." The perpetuation of an I vs. you, we vs. they, in-group vs. out-group mentality can do little for a positive reconstruction of our social reality. Though opposition to an outgroup is an oft-noted means of building support for an in-group's reality, this tactic involves a risk to everyone's reality in the long run.[5]

In place of opposition to an out-group, a pluralistic commune may attempt to increase the sense of community by creating some common task which will help to define the in-group positively rather than negatively: in short, a pluralistic commune may try to become monistic. Though no ideological or religious understanding united its members initially, their primary though still abstract drive toward community may provoke a secondary interest in a common task that would make their sense of community more concrete. Whether they engage in cottage industry or local school work, the important thing is that they are doing something together. Even though they were not brought together as a monistic commune defined by a common interest, they may find the best way of remaining together to be as a monistic commune united by an agreed upon task.

This possibility is not only a real possibility for the pluralistic urban commune; it also describes the actual condition of many non-political, non-religious rural communes where the common task of survival and living on the earth defines the common labor of many. But several reasons lead us to take less interest in the way communes can become more monistic than in the way communes can cope with pluralism. Among these the most pressing is surely our own need to cope within a pluralistic commune. We know less about monistic communes, and we should say correspondingly less about them. But our vindication of the pluralistic commune and relative neglect of the monistic commune should not be taken as an implicit criticism of monistic communes. We simply have more interest in the problems of the pluralistic commune.

A second reason is the suspicion that for most Americans the pluralistic commune is a more likely alternative to present social structures than the monistic commune. Infected more by a lack of community than by a lack of organizations and institutions for channeling their commitments, most Americans would probably be attracted more by the idea of living with a group of *people* than by the idea of joining a cadre for a *cause*.

Third, the problems of pluralism, and the pluralism of the monistic/pluralistic distinction itself, fascinate us for their apparent inevitability. They must be coped with because they will not go away and the attempt to think them away may represent a dangerous rather than a salutary form of utopianism. The monist/pluralist split may be a permanent feature of social dynamics because it follows from a permanent feature of human nature, that tension of opposites most comprehensively referred to by the names Dionysus and Apollo.[6] If each of us is struggling to maintain a balance between unity and order on the one hand and the free and passionate expression of diverse feelings and impulses on the other, then it stands to reason that one person's Apollo may trigger another's Dionysus and vice versa. And once the process has been triggered, the natural dynamic will lead toward accentuation and fixity of the opposition between the persons involved. The self-perpetuating dynamic of the opposition suggests that if the monists in a given commune were to go off and live by themselves, and the pluralists likewise, the same old division would likely crop up anew in each group. This suspicion is corroborated by researches in small-group dynamics.*

One final consideration relates to the way pluralistic communes can utilize contrasts without exploiting them solely for the support of private ideology. As a context for a fluid sorting-out process rather than a medium for uninterrupted support, the pluralistic commune will doubtless reach a point when it has served its purposes and can dissolve. Unlike either marriage or the monistic commune, the pluralistic commune has a half-life built into its very nature. When most of its members have met their challenges or made their discoveries, it has no real reason for further existence. Unlike the monistic commune, it has no *raison d'etre* other than the processes of personal development we have discussed. After those processes have run their course—and we admit that this point in time is not easy to establish, for what is quitting too soon? what is sheer stubbornness?—then the pluralistic commune should serve as an excellent example of the kind of institution Bennis and Slater describe in *The Temporary Society*.[7] It should dissolve itself.

An understanding of the half-life nature of the pluralistic commune is important because without such an understanding dissolution, when it comes, will not come easily. Instead the natural human tendency in the face of dissolution will be to fix the blame for the failure of the "family." Rather than parting as friends who served one another well, the members of the dissolved commune may go their separate ways with resentments and destructive doubts. While the previous argument may constitute a massive rationalization for a dissolution that might be premature, we feel

---

*For research and insights into the way Dionysian, pluralistic influences function positively for the cohesion and equilibrium (and not, as one might suspect, toward the diffusion) of a group, see Robert A. Dentler and Kai T. Erikson, "The Functions of Deviance in Groups," *Social Problems* 7 (1959), 98-107. This study shows not only that deviance is permitted, but that it is induced and sustained by the dynamics of small groups. For complementary researches on the group inducement of Apollonian roles of ordering leadership, see Philip E. Slater, "Role Differentiation in Small Groups," *American Sociological Review* 7 (1955), 300-310; and Slater, *Microcosm* (New York, 1966).

nevertheless that the half-life nature of pluralistic communes is a sound point that follows from the previous arguments.

In order not to let this single point take on too much significance, let us summarize the several theses from which it follows more as a corollary than as a conclusion. We find that the transcendental perspective of the sociology of knowledge offers a powerful tool for understanding contemporary social experience. Taking Berger and Kellner's study of marriage as an initial clue, we have examined the way communes succeed and fail in performing the function of supporting an individual's reality. Though the pluralistic commune appeared doomed to failure on the model of conflict and support implicit in their study, we have argued for a different model, one in which there can be support for some criticism and criticism of some support. The model is complex, but so is life. And even though we balk at the cry, "Long live the pluralistic commune," we know the pluralistic commune as an intensely living experience.

NOTES

1. Peter Berger and Hansfried Kellner, "Marriage and the Construction of Reality," *Diogenes* 46 (1964), 1-25; reprinted in *Recent Sociology*, No. 2, ed. Hans Peter Dreitzel, New York, 1970, pp. 50-72. Our page references (given in parentheses in the text) are to the reprinted edition. As Dreitzel notes in his introduction to "Marriage and the Construction of Reality," the article "was an earlier product of considerations which led to *The Social Construction of Reality; A Treatise in the Sociology of Knowledge* by Berger and Thomas Luckmann (Garden City, New York, 1966). As the latter title indicates, Berger *et al.* are squarely in the tradition from Kant and Hegel through Karl Mannheim. See Mannheim's *Ideology and Utopia*, tr. Wirth and Shils (New York, 1936), and *From Karl Mannheim*, ed. with Introduction by Kurt H. Wolff (New York, 1971).

2. Aristotle, *Nicomachean Ethics*, Bk. I, ch. 9, 1100a1-3.

3. Hegel, *Phenomenology of Mind*, tr. Baillie (New York, 1931), p. 366.

4. C. G. Jung, *Psychological Reflections*, quoted in *The Last Whole Earth Catalogue* (1971), p. 18.

5. Cf. R.D. Laing, *The Politics of the Family*, Massey Lectures on CBC, esp. conclusion; and T. W. Adorno, Else Frenkel-Brunswik, D. J. Levinson, and R. N. Sanford, *The Authoritarian Personality* (New York, 1950).

6. For the richest expressions of the Apollo/Dionysus split in human nature see Nietzsche, *The Birth of Tragedy*, and C. G. Jung, *Psychological Types*, Collected Works, Vol. 6 (Princeton, 1971), pp. 136-46.

7. Warren G. Bennis and Philip E. Slater, *The Temporary Society* (New York, 1968), esp. pp. 127 ff.

THE KIBBUTZIM AND THE SPIRIT OF ISRAEL: AN INTERPRETATIVE ESSAY

DOUGLAS STURM

THE ISRAELI KIBBUTZ has been examined, probed, praised, and criticized by many hands.[1] It has been judged by an economist as "a unique socio-economic structure unparalleled in any other part of the world,"[2] by a sociologist as the "most significant contribution to 'social engineering' in modern times,"[3] and by a political interpreter as "the most imaginative and unique institution of Israel."[4] The last judgment is striking in light of the multiple forms of social experimentation and social invention that pervade Israel's life—the Histadrut, the Jewish National Fund, the Moshavim, Nachal, the Lachish regional development system, and so on. The kibbutzim clearly represent someting of special significance, even though, from a demographic standpoint, they have always constituted but a minority segment of Israeli population and their proportion has been decreasing steadily and appreciably since the War of Independence in 1948.

The purpose of this essay is to suggest that the special significance of the kibbutz movement is located in large part in two motifs that characterize its basic nature. The first motif is the spirit of Israel, the second is the dynamic tension between the practical and the ideal. Thus the first and dominant thesis of the essay is that the kibbutzim represent an effort, perhaps on the part of many kibbutzniks an unwitting effort, to translate the spirit of Israel as a religious community into concrete social, cultural, economic, and political form. The second thesis is that the kibbutzim,

Douglas Sturm, a contributor to *Soundings'* special issue on the philosophy of law in 1968, is professor of religion and political science at Bucknell University. He recently spent time in Israel on grants from the America-Israel Cultural Foundation.

in origin and development, constitute an interplay between pragmatic considerations and utopian vision. In connection with these theses it is further suggested on the one hand that the kibbutz style of living will retain its vitality only to the extent that its members are aware of and are sustained by their religious sources, and on the other hand that the quality of kibbutz life will be preserved only to the extent that the kibbutzniks retain a dynamic and creative tension between their devotion to principle and their openness to adaptation and experimentation. The second thesis is more easily documented than the first. Yet in my judgment the first thesis is the more basic and is that on which the second rests. I must admit at the outset that the overall position I am representing is highly tendentious, for less than 6% of the kibbutzim, calculated according to population, are religious by specific declaration. Virtually all the rest are specifically areligious or even antireligious. Paradoxical as it may sound, however, it is arguable that the repudiation of religion by the secular kibbutzniks in fact permitted a more profound realization of the religious spirit of Israel than was otherwise possible.

Historically, the kibbutz movement is one of the expressions of modern Zionism. In the medieval period the Jews were a pariah people, an extra-territorial people, dispersed among many areas and populations, having a common religious identity rooted in a normative past and pointed toward a messianic future, but within the present suffering from a sense of being unwanted, disliked, exploited, and persecuted, and living largely within ghettos. Whatever may have been the contentment of European Jews in these circumstances, it was disturbed by two countervailing movements during the nineteenth century, the Haskala (enlightenment) movement, which had a modernizing effect upon the Jewish people, and the pogroms and persecutions suffered in Eastern Europe, especially Russia, during the last quarter of the century. Thus arose the Jewish Question: What is the destiny, the purpose, the fate of the Jew in the modern world? What can he do? What ought he do? Among the possibilities open to him within the context of his experience and expectations as Jew, what should be the direction of his life? How can he and how ought he avoid discrimination, escape the ghetto, and live a life of dignity, security, and honor within the modern world?

There were two alternative answers to the Jewish Question: assimilationism and Zionism. The Jew might seek to lose his separate identity as Jew, to become simply a Russian, Pole, German, Englishman, or whatever. But there was always the question whether assimilation was possible, whether others would let him become one of them, or for that matter, whether he could even himself cease being haunted by a sense of belonging to the Jewish people.

Modern Zionism, whose antecedents go back to the sixteenth century, was the other alternative. While modern Zionism consists of both a self-avowed religious and a self-declared secular branch, they are one in seeking an answer to the Jewish Question. The Zionist answer may be encapsulated in the titles of two of the seminal books of the movement—Leo Pinsker's *Autoemanzipation* (1882) and Theodor Herzl's *Der Judenstaat* (1896). Zionism is essentially a liberation movement. The emancipation of the Jews and the solution to the Jewish problem will occur when the Jews, through their own efforts, possess their own land and establish their own state. In Pinsker's words, "The proper and the only remedy [to the Jewish Question] would be the creation of a Jewish nationality, of a people living upon its own soil, the auto-emancipation of the Jews; their emancipation as a nation among other nations by the acquisition of a home of their own."[5] Self-determination, self-reliance, the Jewish people voluntarily and freely creating their own life and shaping their own destiny—these are the qualities that constitute the heart of the Zionism move-ment and that constitute as well one of the primary driving forces of the kibbutzim. As David Ben-Gurion indicated in a speech in 1944, "Galut [i.e., 'exile'] means dependence. . . . Our task is to break radically with this dependence and to become masters of our own fate—in a word, to achieve independence."[6]

The independence of the Jewish people could not, it was de-cided by the Zionist movement, be realized in *any* possible loca-tion. The delegates at the 1903 meeting of the World Zionist Congress vigorously opposed a proposal that the Jews settle in Uganda. The only acceptable location for the new Jewish state was Palestine. The Myth of the Return, as Ferdynand Zweig has ar-gued, is one of the dominant beliefs of the modern Israeli. Self-determination, independence, auto-emancipation—this is possible only by returning to the Land of the Fathers, the Land of the Israelites, the Land in which and on which this People became a People. It is difficult, perhaps impossible, fully to understand the Myth of the Return and the special significance of this Land apart from their religious roots, even while granting the high incidence of agnosticism, atheism, or explicit religious indifference among Zionists. The originating events of this People, the events that make this Land a special Land were theophanous experiences. The history of the Israelites by virtue of which the categories of Exile, Diaspora, and Return make any kind of sense is a history of the interaction between this People and their God.

Under the impetus of the Zionist organization, especially at times of particularly harsh persecution and vivid anti-Semitism, large groups of Jews began in the 1880's to emigrate to Palestine. Many were settled on large farms purchased with funds provided by the Rothschild and the Hirsch families and managed by specially hired professional agronomists. The first kibbutz, Degania Aleph, was formed in 1909 out of reaction against one of these settlements situated in the Jordan Valley, south of Lake Kinneret. A small group within the settlement, rebelling against the arbitrary methods of the manager, received reluctant permission to establish their own farm without administrator, supervisor, or overseer. According to one of the founders, the group was motivated by a number of concerns: "(1) a communal settlement and a way of life based on complete equality; (2) no private ownership of the means of production and no exploitation of labor of one by another; (3) utilization of the production, property and functions of the kibbutz on the principle of 'from each according to his ability and to each according to his needs'; (4) full mutual aid and mutual responsibility to free the individual from worries over his own and his family's existence."[7]

It has been stressed that the founders of the first kibbutz did not imagine themselves to be initiating a new movement. Nor did they approach their new form of settlement with a full-blown plan of organization and procedure. In that sense they were not making an effort to form a "utopian community" or a "perfect society." They were merely being consistent Zionists. Having escaped from the dependency of the Galut, they did not intend to be subjected to a new dependency. The voluntaristic principle was paramount in their rejection both of the Jewish ghetto within a foreign land and of the administered plantation on their own land.

But Zionism was not the only positive influence upon their social ideas and practices. The second most dominant influence was socialism. Most Jewish immigrants during the latter part of the nineteenth century and the early decades of the twientieth century were from Eastern Europe, particularly Russia. In that context, the socialist movement represented the same effort to overcome exploitation, alienation, and dependency as the Zionist movement. One must remember that Moses Hess was at one and the same time an important socialist theoretician of the nineteenth century and an ardent Jewish nationalist. He broke with Marx and Engels on the question of economic determinism, but his humanitarian socialism remained influential within Jewish circles. The difference between Zionism and socialism, as expressed by one kibbutznik, is that while Zionism is the effort of the person as Jew to attain liberation, socialism is the effort of the person as man to attain the same end.[8] Thus the socialist principle is the more universalistic counterpart of the Zionist principle. But neither principle is individualistic. Liberation within these categories of thought does not mean each man going his own way. Quite the contrary, liberation means cooperation, a working together for the mutual benefit of all.

Another of the influences on the gradual development of the kibbutz philosophy and style of life was the youth movements of Europe of the Wandervogel type. The youth movements were characterized by a rejection of traditional forms, an identity with "nature," an intense sense of organic belongingness with each other, a yearning for adventure, a discovery of the sheer joy of working, singing, playing, and wandering together.

With this complex background, the kibbutzim can be understood as expressions of four fundamental principles: (1) the voluntary principle, (2) the communal principle, (3) the equalitarian principle, and (4) the pioneering principle.

(1) In accordance with the voluntary principle, no one is forced to join a kibbutz and anyone who is a member of a kibbutz may resign if and when he wishes. Children are not considered members of a kibbutz. Only after their schooling, and now after their period of initial service in the Israeli army, may they declare their desire and intent to become members. To be accepted they must be approved by a general assembly of the kibbutz they intend to join. Immigrants may seek membership only after a period of "probation," usually a year. The intention is to do everything possible to insure that no one is captive to the kibbutz, even though at the same time, as will be explained later, kibbutz education is designed to demonstrate the superiority of kibbutz living and to acculturate the young to accept and to adopt its pattern.

(2) Henrik Infield, in an early book on the kibbutzim, distinguished between segmental (or partial) cooperation and comprehensive (or all-inclusive) cooperation. Segmental cooperation is limited to specified aims, and thus is quite compatible with competition in other areas; comprehensive cooperation, on the other hand, means that "all the essential interests of life are satisfied in a cooperative way."[9] The kibbutz is an example of comprehensive cooperation. The communal principle is applied to virtually all critical areas of life. It determines the organization of work and production. It governs the property of the kibbutz. With the exception only of a very few personal items, private property is abolished within the kibbutzim. It is employed in the allocation of resources and patterns of consumption. And it is strikingly evident in the manner in which children are raised, trained, and educated. One interpreter is led to remark that the kibbutz movement is "the closest approach to the way of living at which Communism aims."[10] According to conception, the kibbutz is thoroughly collectivistic, but not, it should be stressed, in the sense that individual liberty is extinguished or in the sense that uniformity of action, character, thought, and life style is expected of all members. The collectivism of the kibbutz means rather that the mode of ownership, of decision-making, of production is communal. The structure of the kibbutz is such that individuality is modified by responsibility.

(3) The equalitarian principle arises from the desire to avoid the rigidities of differentiation or super- and sub-ordination according to class lines, sexual difference, birth, or wealth. Initially the principle of equality was applied strictly and directly. It was assumed that anyone could perform any job assignment equally well. Allotments of clothes and food were the same to all. Everyone was eligible for any committee or office that was established. Scrupulous regard was paid to the equality of women in all respects. Over the course of time, however, strict equality was modifed by the Marxist principle which recurs again and again in discussion of kibbutzim, "From each according to his abilities, to each according to his needs." Consequently, whatever distinctions of power, position, privilege, or prestige do exist within the kibbutz, the effort is made to assure that they are understandable and justifiable on the basis of that principle.

(4) The pioneering principle embraces a complex set of factors: a sense of the intrinsic value of labor, a strong attachment

to land and soil, and a readiness to move into circumstances of extreme danger and hardship and to overcome virtually insurmountable obstacles to envisioned goals. From the time of the formation of the first kibbutz over sixty years ago to the present, kibbutzim have been the primary means of land development. They have literally made deserts bloom and marshes produce. They have pushed further and further into areas that to all appearances were uninhabitable and inarable. Furthermore, kibbutzim have been one of the primary instruments of defense on the frontiers of Israel since the War of Independence, and even before 1948 they constituted the major means of maintaining a Jewish presence with force in the Palestinian area. It is instructive to know that one of the first moves of the Israelis in the Golan Heights after the Six-Day War (1967) was to establish a set of kibbutzim in the area.

The attachment to land, the focus on agricultural work constituted a deliberate break with the Jewish existence of the shtetl, the Eastern European Jewish village in which the Jew was the lender of money, the keeper of shops, the economic middleman. But a nation cannot be built on economic middlemen. Indeed, it was argued, the re-formation of the Jewish nation requires a return to the soil, a direct dealing with the natural context of life. The Jew must once again become a tiller of the soil, such that he genuinely belongs to the land and the land belongs to him.

The strong attachment to land and soil that characterized the impetus of the Zionist movement in general and the kibbutz movement in particular is conjoined with a conviction of the intrinsic value of labor. Both of these aspects of the pioneering principle were expressed directly, forcefully, and influentially by Aaron D. Gordon, a Russian who "returned" to Palestine to become a laborer on the land and who spent his last days on Degania, the first kibbutz. In 1911 he wrote, "In Palestine we must do with our own hands all the things that make up the sum total of life. We must ourselves do all the work, from the least strenuous, cleanest, and most sophisticated, to the dirtiest and most difficult. In our own way, we must feel what a worker feels and think what a worker thinks. . . . From now on our principal ideal must be Labor. . . . The ideal of Labor must become the pivot of all our aspirations. . . . What we need is zealots of Labor."[11]

It was Gordon's argument that only through labor can a man become one with himself and with his natural and social context.

Labor is a creative act wherein nature and man are drawn together in a new identity. This orientation entails a radical reversal of the prevailing Western notion that correlates prestige with white collar work and administration. Indeed, within the kibbutzim the pioneering principle means rejecting hired labor, for to hire another is to exploit him. The basic assumption is, of course, the Marxist-socialist theory of surplus value.

In sum, the basic vision of the kibbutz arose out of a complex set of influences—Zionism, socialism, youth movements—all reactions against exploitation, authoritarianism, and the narrow confines of ghetto existence. In positive form, the vision of the kibbutz is a construct of four principles—the voluntaristic, the communal, the equalitarian, and the pioneering principles. Over the course of the past six decades the vision seems to have remained much the same, but the precise form of realization has varied more or less depending upon social context and depending on the challenges presented to the movement.

Note, for instance, the origins of one of the most carefully and thoroughly investigated aspects of kibbutz life, namely, collective education. The members of the first kibbutz had given no thought to the structure and development of education that would be in keeping with their convictions. The problem was confronted only with the birth of children. The primary desire of the women who had given birth was to retain their status of equality with men and not to be forced into the traditional Western mold of housekeeper, kitchen worker, and child-raiser. The question of what to do with and for the children became a matter of serious debate within the individual kibbutzim and at conventions of women workers. The matter became resolved in principle only after several years, when it was determined that the children should be raised and educated in communal fashion.

While there are some variations in detail and changes are constantly effected, the basic pattern of child development and education is the same in all kibbutzim. The heart of the educational system is the children's house and the children's society. While continuing to stress the family relationship as a companionship unit, the kibbutz, in establishing a set of children's houses differentiated according to age, aspires to abolish the patriarchal authority of the father, to overcome the usual social constraints and limitations that accompany motherhood, and to provide a means of actualizing the communal style of life of the kibbutz for children at the very beginning. There are five stages of houses—infants' (birth to fifteen months), toddlers' (fifteen months to four years), kindergarten (four years to seven years), children's (seven years to twelve years), and high school (twelve years to eighteen years). In each house, there are trained personnel (metaplot) who are responsible for the physical care and welfare of the children, who provide affection, comfort, and love, who train the children, and who constitute basic socializers in the values of the kibbutz. Besides the metaplot there are teachers and educators in the kindergarten, children's house, and high school. With few exceptions all personnel are members of the kibbutz. There is a period of time, two or three hours, during which parents and children are together each day, a period that is intense, concentrated, and highly cherished. In this sytem, the child from birth not only interacts with a number of adults who fulfill significant roles in relation to him (a process sometimes called "multiple mothering"); he is also led to depend on, to support, to seek assistance from, and to sense his participation in his peer group. There is no "only child" in the kibbutz. Nor is there, in a sense, any "lonely child" in the kibbutz.

In both primary and secondary school the kibbutz is taken as a model, in the sense that the boys and girls organize their own society with committees to plan and to conduct special activities for the entire group, and all are expected to assume work assignments on the children's farm, at a special training farm, or, in the case of the oldest children, on the regular kibbutz farm. Thus the principles of kibbutz life constituted the basis for constructing the framework for the pattern of child care and education.

The pattern is not static, however. Many educational issues are currently under debate in the kibbutzim, ranging from whether the youngest children should sleep in their parents' quarters for a greater sense of security to the question of how to provide the specialized university education needed in an advancing industrialized society while preserving the values of kibbutz life. The point is that the kibbutzim did not originate with a rigid or set blueprint of collective education. The pattern gradually was formed, given, on the one side, the fundamental principles of the kibbutz movement and, on the other side, the necessity of assuming responsibility for the education of children. The kibbutzim seem, furthermore, to be open to a continuing reform of the educational process as it seems necessary or desirable given new research or new circumstances. For this reason the major federations of the kibbutzim in Israel have established centers for research and training in child development and education.[12]

It is asserted again and again that the major objective of the kibbutz method of training and educating children is to ensure the preservation and continuance of the kibbutz. According to one interpreter[13] the collective educational scheme can be adjudged a partial success on these grounds. In his investigation of kibbutzniks who have been raised and educated through the system, the majority view the kibbutz as the most desirable form of social life. They find security within the group and have no striving for a different or "higher" status. They value work, especially physical work, highly. They accept the principle of collective ownership. Yet their adoption and acceptance of the kibbutz way of life is not uncritical or unmodified. The general lack of privacy is a source of frustration. They are motivated to work not so much out of a sense of creative vocation as out of a consciousness of responsibility to the group or desire for prestige. They lack the ideological fervor of the founders of the kibbutz. While strongly loyal to Israel as a Jewish state, they are not as devoted as the original Zionists to Jewish culture and history as such. Because the educational system is oriented so directly to the necessities and values of the kibbutz, some feel it is too restrictive, not providing, for instance, the optimal conditions needed to develop artistic talent or specialized intellectual interests. Yet overall the sabras born and educated in the communal setting seem to find the kibbutz style of life rewarding. One possible, although not altogether unambiguous, index of this is the calculation that between 80% and 90% remain within the kibbutz movement after their period of military service.

The kibbutzim were by origin and remain predominantly (though not without appreciable change) agricultural in character. The agricultural concentration was a matter both of principle and need. On the one hand, only through agriculture was it possible to interact directly and creatively with the land, and this is one facet of the pioneering principle of the kibbutz movement. On the other hand, only through extensive land development was it possible to work toward a viable Jewish state. Thus with land and capital provided on a low-cost and long-term basis, the kibbutzim set out to cultivate areas that appeared absolutely barren. But in doing so, the effort was (and is) made to apply the communal principle to all aspects of the economic process—in production and in consumption. Furthermore, the effort was (and is) made to plan, administer, and conduct the economic process within the full context of kibbutz life. Thus profit maximization has not been the sole or even the primary consideration governing the process. One of the most important considerations that affect the kibbutz economy is its contribution to the national purposes of the Israeli people. This explains their willingness to move into areas that persons and groups concerned first and foremost with profits avoid with scarcely a single glance, and it explains as well their readiness to undertake the burdens of security costs and of guarding the borders of the nation. Another consideration affecting the kibbutz economy is the determination to provide optimal services and decent standards of living for the entire kibbutz population. This consideration enters into the allocation of personnel and the manner in which the income of the kibbutz is distributed. In fact, consumption norms are often defined and set as guides independently of and prior to concerns of production and profit. On balance, concern for the welfare of the kibbutz community and Israeli society surpass the matter of profitability as economic criteria, while at the same time, given the desire to create a self-sustaining community, the kibbutz does not ignore the need to assure the profitable character of its enterprises.

Within the agricultural sector the kibbutzim have been unusually productive, showing a higher rate of growth in dairy products, poultry, field crops, and other areas than the rest of Israel's agriculture. In 1963, for instance, although only 18.7% of the agricultural labor force of Israel were on kibbutzim, the kibbutz movement accounted for one third of Israel's total agricultural production. Their relatively high rate of productivity is the result of their readiness to exploit the most modern techniques and mechanized instruments of farming. However, productivity and profitability are not the same, and the kibbutz movement often shows losses at the conclusion of a year for many reasons—their locations result in higher security and marketing costs; they engage in diversified farming as a matter of principle; a percentage of their members is on call to work full time for the federations of kibbutzim or the labor and political organizations to which the kibbutzim belong; federations of kibbutzim rarely dissolve any of their units despite economic difficulty, with the result that the overall profitability of the kibbutzim is lowered; and so on.[14]

Despite the high value placed on labor connected directly with the land, the kibbutz movement has been developing manufacturing establishments and industrial enterprises. Various reasons for this development have been put forward: the need to provide productive work for persons not fit for agricultural assignments, the desire to provide a greater diversity of skilled occupations for the members of the kibbutz, a response to the general trend toward industrialization within Israeli society, the need to stabilize income given the fluctuations, seasonal and cyclical, in agriculture, the decreased number of labor days required for agricultural production given the technological revolution, and the desire to enhance the overall profitability of the kibbutz economy.

The trend toward greater sophistication and mechanization in agricultural production and toward the incorporation of industrial enterprises into the kibbutz economy have resulted in serious discussion about whether the kibbutz movement is remaining true to its originating principles. As I have already observed, both of these trends result in increasing the distance between the laboring person and the land. In addition, they both require a high degree of specialized graining and expert management, resulting in a division of labor that threatens the principle of equality. Because of a perennial manpower shortage, furthermore, kibbutzim have been forced to hire outside labor despite their convictions against labor exploitation. Finally, it is suspected that the communal character and the simplicity of life that constituted the early kibbutzim will be destroyed by the necessity for long-range technical planning and use of experts.

Yet it might be argued that the very fact that the kibbutzim are aware of the problem and that the federations of the kibbutzim are seeking methods of organizing and conducting the industries to minimize bureaucracy, to secure wide participation in the formation of policies, and to provide full benefits to laborers hired from outside the kibbutz (as well as inviting them to join the kibbutz itself) will at least assist in minimizing the danger that the principles of the kibbutz will be violated by these developments. It is possible to discern within the kibbutz movement at this time a serious effort at one and the same time to move along with economic developments in Israel and to maintain the fundamental principles of the kibbutzim. Without modernization and industrialization the kibbutz would no longer be a viable style of life, or at the least it would become an isolated and completely insignificant pocket of curiosity, contrary to its Zionist-socialist origins. One of the most serious questions confronting the kibbutz movement is how to institutionalize its principles within a modern economy.

The communal dining room and the communal laundry are symbols, even if not fully sufficient symbols, of the embodiment of the principles of the kibbutz in procedures of economic distribution and consumption. The kibbutz as a unit provides all the goods and services required by its members. Food, clothing, housing, personal items, entertainment, education, health care, transportation, vacations, whatever—are all furnished by the kibbutz. In the early years the standard of living was exceedingly low and the style of life had an ascetic, almost puritanically simple character about it. All goods were considered fully communal, including clothing. Since then the pattern, standard, and style have changed considerably, partially because of economic growth, partially in response to competition with modern styles of life in the surrounding urban culture, and partially as a result of a growing conviction about the value of individuality, privacy, and personal differences. "The introduction of the first electric tea kettle and the first radio in the homes of some members [as personal gifts from friends outside the kibbutz] produced a terrific furor. They were condemned as the cause of two major sins against kibbutz ideology: they brought ownership of private property into the kibbutz, which was strictly prohibited, and they upset the principle of equality. . . . The problem was finally solved by a decision to provide all members with an electric tea kettle and a radio."[15] Now it is common for each housing unit to have its own air conditioner, refrigerator, stove, collection of books, and record player, and for each single member or married couple to have an automobile and some regular allocation of funds to use at their own discretion. The communal dining room is still central, however, and all decisions about allocation of resources are determined by the community in assembly.

According to one veteran kibbutznik,[16] the kibbutz has solved the problem of equality and sufficiency of physical goods. It has overcome the injustices of maldistribution and provides a comfortable standard of physical existence. Its primary economic problem now is that of accommodating to individual differences and fulfilling the higher aspirations of the human spirit. Is it possible for the kibbutz adequately to provide for the philosopher, the astronomer, the artist, the poet? Kibbutzim do in fact make provisions for artists and writers, and do support special training and advanced education for those members who appear to have the potentiality to benefit therefrom, but the question remains to what extent and with what limits the principles of kibbutz life are compatible with individual creativity, divergence of thought and action, and work that may not be profitable or productive in the usual economic sense. Can the kibbutz support those forms of individual creative activity that consume one's time and energy but whose worth cannot be calculated on an accountant's ledger? Is it feasible to support the specialized education of someone when it seems clear that the result will not contribute to the kibbutz and that the person educated will most likely be led to seek a position outside it? These questions are critical both in relation to the internal policies of the kibbutz movement and, more important, in relation to the role of the kibbutz in the larger political and cultural society of Israel.

Politically, the kibbutz was organized in the beginning as closely as possible in conformity with the principles of direct and pure democracy. All basic decisions were made by an assembly of all the members, meeting once a week. Matters of economic production and consumption, time schedules, housing and eating arrangements were all brought before the assembly. Even yet the assembly is the supreme authority in each local kibbutz. But the actual process of decision-making has been modified appreciably in two ways. First, as the kibbutz economy has become increasingly sophisticated technologically, some members have simply become more knowledgeable and proficient in certain areas than others. Their authoritativeness has been acknowledged, and often they are given special positions. Thus the accountant's position within the kibbutz is not and can not be open for any one. It requires special preparation. The kibbutz, furthermore, has had to shift from ad hoc, on the spot decision-making to long-range calculations, cost/benefit analyses, and other forms of complex administrative projections. On most kibbutzim either a secretariat or some type of executive committee has been established as an intermediate body between the general assembly on the one hand and the various branches of the kibbutz economy with their committees formed for special purposes—cultural, educational, and social as well as economic—on the other. While the general assembly retains its position as the supreme authority in policy matters, its actual power and control have been severely modified through this more complex organizational structure, which in turn arose out of a response to the sheer necessities of social and economic development. Of course, it must be noted that the membership of each of the almost 250 kibbutzim is fairly limited in size, from about 60 to about 1000, and averaging about 350. Thus even with some degree of complexity in organization and operation it is possible for all members to have some acquaintance with the entire system of the kibbutz.

The process of open democratic decision-making has been modified as well by other basic changes in the organization of the kibbutz. Virtually all the kibbutzim have been organized into federations, which in turn are affiliated with various political parties. Furthermore, most of the kibbutzim are members of the Histadrut, the Israeli labor organization which not only serves as a regular trade union but also provides extensive social services, owns some of the major industrial enterprises in Israel, and operates a major marketing agency and wholesale cooperative. Thus the kibbutzim are tied into organizations of national scope from which they benefit but to which they are to some degree responsible. One federation contains twenty departments covering various aspects of kibbutz life—education, finance, water, agricultural planning and research, culture, security, industry, etc. Each department has its own staff and provides assistance to kibbutzim that need help, but it also establishes norms and standards for individual kibbutzim. The federation further is responsible for new settlements, mutual aid among and between established kibbutzim, representation of the kibbutzim in national bodies—the Histadrut, government agencies, national and international Jewish organizations—and liaison with the political party with which it is affiliated.

Thus the individual kibbutz is not a small, isolated, self-contained rural collective. It is tied into a network of associations which on the one side increases its potential influence and impact on Israel's life, but on the other side heavily compromises the apparently rather simple democratic style of its origins. Its national associations affect both its policies and its personnel. In matters of policy the federation has final authority on matters of basic principle, and at times in the history of the kibbutz movement this has resulted in severe friction and clash. With respect to personnel, it is significant that from 6% to 10% of the members of the kibbutz movement work outside the kibbutz to which they belong. They may be officials in the federation, their political party, or the Histadrut. They may hold local or national political office. They may be in the army. They may have assumed posts in manufacturing enterprises or financial institutions connected with the labor organization or owned and managed by a regional association of kibbutzim. Indeed, a highly significant proportion of the leadership of Israeli society has come out of and is still associated with the kibbutz movement, far surpassing their proportion within the entire population. In 1960, when the kibbutz population constituted only 4.21% of Israel, 18% of the members of Knesset, the Israeli parliament, were past or current members of kibbutzim. In 1965, when the kibbutz popularion stood at 3.82% of the Jewish population in Israel, 14% of the representatives in Knesset were from kibbutzim. Exactly why members of kibbutzim occupy elitist-leadership positions within Israeli society out of proportion to their actual numbers and exactly what difference it makes and will continue to make in the quality and direction of Israeli life is an open and difficult question.

However, so far as the import of this fact is concerned, the answer is clear. If one examines the kibbutz movement only superficially it has the appearance of a sectarian group. Indeed, it has been compared historically to the Essenes and the Qumran settlement. But if it is sectarian in the character or quality of its communal life, it is not the kind of sectarianism that seeks to lead a pure life withdrawn from the rest of humanity. It is instead a sectarianism of a transformative character. The kibbutzim not only permit but encourage and pledge a significant number of their members to work and to assume positions of leadership outside the community in order to have a transformative impact upon Israeli society as a whole and in the final analysis upon the entire world of mankind. As one kibbutznik wrote recently, "the criterion of kibbutz success cannot be measured only in its ability to provide a finer and juster way of life for its members, but no less in its role in the major processes of Zionist realization and class struggle."[17] The fundamental vision of the kibbutz movement is in effect of a new heaven and a new earth, or more modestly, of a new society and a new man. This is the vision that arises out of the influences from whose combination the movement emerged—particularly Zionism and socialism. These "isms" are retained as part of the basic belief structure and mythology of the most dedicated kibbutzniks even while a significant number of younger members of the kibbutzim are more or less cynical about the ideology and more pragmatic in orienation.

This brings me back to the theses articulated in the opening passages of this essay. It seems clear that over the course of six decades there have been appreciable changes in kibbutz life in all areas—educational, economic, and political. The changes, furthermore, have been largely deliberate. There has been an explicit effort to take account of the shifting social, cultural, and economic environment within which the kibbutzim exist and to adapt, without compromise, the basic principles of the movement to these circumstances; that is, the effort has been made to maintain a voluntaristic, communal, equalitarian, and pioneering social pattern even while creating a more mechanized, complex, highly organized, and technologically sophisticated system. The attempt to remain true to these principles and to the formative influences underlying them—Zionism and socialism—is, as might be expected, more characteristic of some kibbutzniks than others, and, according to some interpreters, more characteristic of the few explicitly religious kibbutzim and the most left-wing federation of kibbutzim (Hakibbutz Haartzi Hashomer Hatzair) than the others.[18] But the point remains that in basic impetus the kibbutz movement is not separatistic.

This means, on the one hand, that the values that constitute its fundamental commitment are not conceived to be merely private, personal, subjective, meant for kibbutzniks alone. They are conceived rather to be the values of man's humanity. From the perspective of the kibbutz movement, freedom, community, equality, labor are the qualities that must determine the basic structure of civilization if civilization is to be genuinely humane. To the extent to which social institutions are not expressive of these qualities they are inhuman and result in alienation, exploitation, and the perversion of man's essential structure.

But to say that in basic impetus the kibbutz movement is not separatistic is also to indicate that, if that impetus is to be retained, the movement must be responsive to social and cultural trends. There is a realistic dimension to both socialism and Zionism which forces one's attention to the developments and processes that are determinative of the actual quality of human existence. Were the kibbutzim to ignore these developments in Israeli life or in the world at large, they would become hopelessly anachronistic. But, of course, simply to capitulate to these developments uncritically, to become in simple fashion pragmatic, and to ignore the basic and informative principles of kibbutz life would be to violate the vision of the new society that gives the kibbutz movement its drive and makes it the unique institution that it has been and is.

Whether or for how long a vital dialectic between the originating and fundamental vision and the actual developments of history and culture can be maintained within kibbutz life is an open question. According to some interpreters, the kibbutz movement is already in decline, both quantitatively and qualitatively. Martin Buber is quoted as observing, "In the course of time the hopes and dreams vanished. It is as if the ideology faded and withered. It seems as if this freshness of life has been cut off from the Kibbutz Movement."[19] Ferdynand Zweig ascribes the decline to a number of factors: the general routinization and aging of the institution, the growth of capital and managerial complexity, loss of enthusiasm for socialism, the actual formation of the Israeli state which has taken away from the importance of voluntary Jewish organizations, the rise of affluence, the trend toward occupations and roles requiring special intellectual training, political conflicts within the kibbutz movement, the decline of agriculture, and the increased proportion of immigration by oriental Jews whose cultural background is significantly different from the European Jews who constitute the basic population of the kibbutzim. To the extent to which Zweig's interpretation is accurate, the tension between the visionary and the pragmatic is reduced, and the special significance of the kibbutz movement is diminishing.

At this point, the first and the more tendentious thesis articulated in the early passages of this essay must be recalled, namely, that the ground of the kibbutzim is the religious spirit of Israel, that the kibbutzim can be understood as an effort to translate the spirit of Israel as a religious community into concrete social, cultural, economic, and political form, and that the kibbutz style of living will retain its vitality only to the extent that its members are aware of and sustained by their religious source. Clearly the main force of the Zionist movement in general, and the vast majority of the pioneers who founded and developed the kibbutz movement in particular, were avowedly antireligious. But the religion they rejected was the religion of the Galut, the religion of the shtetl, the narrow orthodoxy that had tended in its own way to neglect the full significance of the religious relation. The rejection was understandable, perhaps even necessary, for the fulfillment of Zionist hopes. It is of interest to note that Rabbi Abraham Isaac Kook, who emigrated to Palestine from Eastern Europe in 1904, served as Chief Rabbi for the occidental Jewish community in Palestine under the British Mandate from 1919 to 1935, and was one of the acknowledged leaders of the religious Zionists, "saw the discarding of religion by [the] pioneers as an inevitable element in the much desired revolution in Jewish life. Rabbi Kook recognized that *galut* had destroyed the Jews' healthy, earthy components."[21] Zionism was the effort to actualize in as full form as possible a dimension of Judaism that was not totally absent from but that was hidden, neglected, obscured, deemphasized in the Judaism of the Galut. The theophanous event that constituted the origin of the Israeli people consisted of certain polarities and tensions—between the transcendent and the immanent, the universal and the particular, the cosmic and the historical, homogeneity and heterogeneity, the inclusive and the exclusive, the divine and the human. The Zionists were concerned to establish a national home, a Jewish state. They opted in the dialectic of history for the immanental, the particular, the human; to secular Zionists the Jewish religion as such was an obstacle, for in their eyes its focus was on the transcendent, the cosmic, the divine, and that, to them, was irrelevant to their enterprise.

One of the major questions to ask of Israel at the present time is whether in creating a nation-state it will become merely a nation among other nations, thus dissolving the tensions and polarities that constitute its full Jewish heritage. The same question can be asked of the kibbutz movement. By origin and intent the kibbutz movement is an earnest of a new epoch in human relations, an influential moment in the history of human becoming, first in Israel (hence its Zionist background) and ultimately among all humanity (hence its socialist background). But whether in actual fact it will continue to function in this manner depends in large part upon whether its members will or can retain a sense of the tension between the visionary and the pragmatic, and this in turn depends upon whether they will or can recover a sense of the polarities of the theophanous event.

According to Zweig, one of the lessons of the kibbutz experience is that "the force of technology and economics is far stronger than that of ideology,"[22] and that is probably true so far as (a) no effort is made to conjoin the ideological factor and technological-economic development in ever new creative form, and so far as (b) the ideological factor is simply that, a set of ideas thought by the mind of man and projected as interesting, desirable, but abstract values. However, the spirit of Israel is after all the spirit of the living God who engages in continuous struggling with man (hence the name "Israel"). It can be argued that the grounding of the Zionist-socialist movement as represented in principle in the kibbutz movement is not fundamentally a set of interesting but abstract ideas that can be given or taken at will and depend for their vitality simply upon cultural circumstance. It can be argued that, from the standpoint of the innermost meaning of Jewish history, the grounding of the movement is that ultimate reality present in all circumstances, calling man to become himself. Thus so far as the basic principles of the kibbutz movement—the voluntaristic, communal, equalitarian, and pioneering principles—are conceived to be ideological abstractions they will be subject to the push and pull of other historical forces, and one suspects that the kibbutz movement will eventually become past history. But so far as the principles are understood as expressions of the ultimate reality that is engaged in continuous struggle with mankind throughout each epoch of history, then the kibbutzim may indeed retain their vitality and special significance not only for Israel but also for all human civilization.

NOTES

1. The research for this essay was supported by grants from Philip Berman, through the America-Israel Cultural Foundation, and from Bucknell University's Ford Foundation Grant for Faculty Development in the Humanities.
2. Eliyahu Kanovsky, *The Economy of the Israeli Kibbutz* (Cambridge, Mass., 1966), p. 3.
3. Ferdynand Zweig, *Israel: The Sword and the Harp* (London, 1969), p. 151.
4. Boris Stern, *The Kibbutz That Was* (Washington, 1965), p. vi.
5. Leo Pinsker, *Auto-Emancipation: An Appeal to His People by a Russian Jew* (1882) in *The Zionist Idea: A Historical Analysis and Reader*, ed. Arthur Hertzberg (Garden City, New York, 1959), p. 198.
6. David Ben-Gurion, "The Imperatives of the Jewish Revolution," in *The Zionist Idea*, p. 609.
7. Stern, p. 7.
8. This was expressed in personal conversation with Chaim Ber of Kibbutz Hagoshrim. See also Melford E. Spiro, *Kibbutz: Venture in Utopia* (Cambridge, Mass., 1956), p. 32.

9. Henrik F. Infield, *Cooperative Living in Palestine* (New York, 1944), p. 20.
10. Georges Friedmann, *The End of the Jewish People?* quoted in Dan Leon, *The Kibbutz: A New Way of Life* (Oxford, 1969), p. 1.
11. Aaron David Gordon, "Some Observations" (1911), in *The Zionist Idea*, p. 374.
12. For an example of the kind of work being done in this area, see *Children in Collectives: Child-rearing Aims and Practices in the Kibbutz*, ed. Peter B. Neubauer (Springfield, Ill., 1965). This volume is a report of an institute held at Oranim Child Guidance Clinic in Kiryat-Tivon, Israel.
13. Melford Spiro, *Children of the Kibbutz* (Cambridge, Mass., 1958), Ch. 14, especially pp. 358-398.
14. See Kanovsky, Chs. VI and VII.
15. Stern, pp. 57f.
16. This was expressed in a personal conversation with Chaim Ber of Kibbutz Hagoshrim.
17. Leon, p. 180.
18. Spiro, *Kibbutz*, pp. 196-197.
19. Quoted in Zweig, p. 158.
20. Zweig, pp. 158-166.
21. Pinchas H. Peli, *Israel: The Religious Dimension* (The Jewish Orientation Fellowship, c. 1969), p. 22.
22. Zweig, p. 165.

COLERIDGE'S UTOPIA REVISITED

CLARKE GARRETT

THE DESIGNING OF communes and utopian societies seems to run in cycles in Western culture. So far, at least, the greatest wave of interest in them came in the period between the 1790's and the 1840's. Inspired in part by the sense of human perfectibility that the Enlightenment and the French Revolution aroused, groups of men, especially young men, came together, talked, and made plans to establish new societies that would not only be free from the inequalities and the corruptions of the old, but would also somehow initiate the regeneration of mankind. They went out sometimes into the American wilderness, sometimes merely to an abandoned farm somewhere. Far more often, the projects never became more than talk.

It is clear that we are now in a similar cycle of interest in "getting back together," to borrow the title of Robert Houriet's excellent book, and it may be that this cycle will prove to be more lasting than was the one in the early nineteenth century. I am hesitant to draw very many parallels between then and now, since such comparisons tend to be either strained or obvious. But it is undeniable that, at least among historians, the·utopian projects and attitudes of the past that were ridiculed a generation ago as foolish and unrealistic are beginning to receive a certain amount of sympathetic attention.

One such communal experiment was the one that the young poets Samuel Taylor Coleridge and Robert Southey, together with several of their friends, intended to establish on the banks of the

Clarke Garrett, an associate professor of history at Dickinson College in Carlisle, Pa., is completing a book on millenarianism in Britain and France during the French Revolution.

Susquehanna River in 1795. Coleridge, the classical scholar, named it Pantisocracy. The project never got beyond the talking stage, but both Southey and Coleridge testified in later life to the immense influence that it had had on their intellectual development.

Pantisocracy began in June of 1794, when Coleridge stopped off at Oxford before he and a Cambridge friend began a walking tour of Wales. Coleridge had resumed his studies at Cambridge two months before, following a brief and unhappy enlistment in the army. At Oxford he visited a friend from his days at Christ's Hospital School in London, Robert Allen. Allen, a pre-medical student, introduced him to a new friend he had met at the anatomy lectures, a sometime poet from Bristol named Robert Southey. The oldest son of a bankrupt merchant whose widow now ran a boarding house, Southey had for some time contemplated, rhetorically but still more or less sincerely, emigration to America. His sole comfort in his present situation, he had written to a friend, lay in contemplating the exciting successes of the French Revolutionary cause: "How much happier should I feel were I on the frontiers of France every hour expos'd to death in a cause I must feel to be just."[1]

What is a liberal arts degree good for? he asked, and college students have echoed him ever since. The only profession he could even consider entering would be medicine, because there at least he could try to serve society.

That was not really a satisfactory alternative either, and two weeks before Coleridge's arrival he had written his oldest friend that either he should secure a government post for himself (impossible, he soon learned, because of his Jacobin politics) or "I quit the country—my friends—and every fondest hope to indulge for ever. . . . If despair be my food I will feed on it in a country where neither my name nor life can be known and where in the society of mechanics I may gradually forget that I was ever qualified for or accustomed to a higher situation."

Then Southey met Coleridge, and Pantisocracy was born. Southey recalled forty-two years later that it had been he and another Oxford friend, George Burnett, who talked the project into shape while Coleridge and his friend were walking through Wales. After his tour Coleridge arrived unexpectedly at Southey's house in Bristol and stayed three weeks, and "then it was that we resolved upon going to America." They set out on foot to visit

Burnett at his father's country estate and tell him the good news. They also stopped at the home of an acquaintance of Coleridge's, a prosperous tanner named Thomas Poole. Poole's letter describing the Pantisocracy project as it was originally conceived, written a month later, is by far the most clear and succinct description that has survived: "Twelve gentlemen of good education and liberal principles are to embark with twelve ladies in April next," first having become as well acquainted as possible and having settled "every regulation of their future conduct. Their opinion was that they should fix themselves at—I do not recollect the place, but somewhere in a delightful part of the new back settlement; that each man should labour two or three hours a day, the produce of which labour would, they imagine, be more than sufficient to support the colony." The produce would be stored and shared out communally. They would assemble a good library and spend their leisure "in study, liberal discussions, and the education of their children." The women would care for the children and engage in "other occupations suited to their strength; at the same time the greatest attention is to be paid to the cultivation of their minds." All members would be free to hold whatever political or religious opinions that they pleased. Anyone could withdraw from "the society" whenever he chose.[2]

The intentional community that Coleridge dubbed Pantisocracy was never established. Within weeks of their visit to Thomas Poole it changed radically, mainly at Southey's instigation. A number of other people had been added, including his mother, his cousin, his brothers, and his future mother-in-law and brothers-in-law. By October, Southey could report to his brother Thomas that "we are now twenty-seven adventurers," and he was talking to six more prospects. At the end of 1794, while Coleridge was in London talking about the project and making inquiries concerning the expenses of transportation to and land purchase in America, the Bristol Pantisocrats decided to launch the communal experiment in Wales first. Coleridge objected, then yielded, but it is clear from his letters that while his interest in Pantisocracy had not diminished, he had some hesitation about its practicability at the present time and with the present companions, particularly with his chosen mate, Sara Fricker, sister of Southey's intended.

In August of 1795, precisely a year after the project was first fully worked out, it collapsed amidst bitterness and recriminations when Southey decided to accompany his uncle to Portugal, vaguely promising to join Pantisocracy in fourteen years. Coleridge married Sara Fricker, and after a honeymoon in the country and a sojourn in Bristol he moved with his wife and infant son, not to America, but to Nether Stowey in Somersetshire, near his friend Thomas Poole, who he hoped would instruct him in agriculture. While the rest of his time would be spent in literary pursuits and the education of his child. Thus the spirit of Pantisocracy lived on even if the reality had died.

Everything in this brief account of Pantisocracy will be familiar to anybody who had read much about the English Romantics. The biographies of the two poets discuss the episode in considerable detail, and in addition there have appeared a number of articles on Pantisocracy over the years, most of them concerned with the literary sources of the project.[3] Given the substantial amount of attention that Pantisocracy has received, another visit to that first of Coleridge's many uncompleted projects might seem to be entirely unnecessary. I would suggest two reasons that Pantisocracy deserves more examination.

In the first place, the collecting and editing of Coleridge materials has become a veritable industry in recent years. Editions of his letters, his notebooks, and his published works are all in progress,[4] and they have generated a revived interest in the poet. One result has been to see the young Coleridge in a somewhat different light. He was more deeply affected by the political, social, and religious tensions of the 1790's than has often been supposed, and the solutions which he sketched out in his published and unpublished writings were more radical.

In the second place, living as we do in an era when the possibility of devising alternative societies to our own receives considerably more sympathetic attention than it used to, Coleridge's ideas are of particular interest. In Pantisocracy, unlike most communal experiments, the traditional family structure was to be maintained. Marriage and family life, in fact, was to be the cement that held the community together.

In the course of planning his community in America, Coleridge began to think about some of the themes that would recur in his writings for the rest of his life. In the disillusionment and sickness of his later years he looked back on the period of Pantisocracy with continued fondness. He wrote that "For a few months America really inspired Hope, and I became an exalted Being." It was the working out of his ideas on Pantisocracy, he wrote in *The*

Friend in 1809, to which he owed "much of whatever I at present possess, my clearest insight into the nature of individual man, and my most comprehensive views of his social relations." Even while seeming to dismiss the plan as "harmless" and "extravagant" and his youthful political radicalism as "the drivel of a Babe," he continued to feel that the premises of Pantisocracy were sound. A truly human community was to be built on three bases: marriage and family life; education; and a Gospel-based religion that had at its core the abolition of private property.

I propose to discuss the three bases of Pantisocracy as Coleridge dealt with them in his writings. It should be emphasized at the outset that I run the danger of reading too much into the scattered comments that are to be found in his works, mainly in those dating from 1795. Also, the interpretation that follows rests on two assumptions. First, I believe that Coleridge did not repudiate his earlier beliefs to the extent that is usually supposed, and therefore his later writings can cast some light on his letters, poems, and lectures of 1795.[5] Second, Coleridge's often distinctive terminology (witness "pantisocracy") masks conceptions and attitudes that he shared with many others of his generation.

His later reflections on Pantisocracy were epitomized in a letter he wrote in 1803: "Our little society, in its second generation was to have combined the innocence of the patriarchal age with the knowledge and genuine refinements of European culture."

He contemplated a sort of two-fold reformation on the part of the Pantisocrats. In the first place, they would commit themselves to the inculcation of duty and benevolence and morality before they entered the community. Once the community had been formed, these attributes would be further intensified, primarily through the experience of marriage and family love. It was "the filial & maternal Affection & Duties," he wrote Southey late in 1794, "which makes Man a little lower than the Angels." When he realized in December that the American project was probably doomed, in part because of Southey's commitments to his own relatives and to the Fricker family, Coleridge, who felt no such attachment to his own kin, wrote:

> Domestic Happiness is the greatest of things sublunary . . . but it is not strange that those things, which in a pure form of Society will constitute its first blessings, should form in it's present morbid state, be our most perilous Temptations—!—'He that doth not love Mother & Wife less than me, is not worthy of me!'

When he wrote in 1803 that he had been "disgusted beyond measure by the manners & morals of the Democrats," he was thinking above all of William Godwin, who in *Political Justice* had derided marriage and advocated sexual promiscuity. In the lectures that Coleridge delivered at Bristol in 1795, he said of the book that whatever was good in it had been better expressed in the Gospels, and "whatever is new is absurd." He extolled the "mild" yet "severe" doctrines of Jesus and quoted the saying, "He that looketh at a married woman to lust after her hath already committed adultery in his heart." Then, thinking perhaps of Pantisocracy, Coleridge concluded: "He demanded from his Disciples a total annihilation of all merely selfish Passions—and enforced an ardent benevolence and the preservation of perfect Equality among ourselves." In his notebooks, two notations concerning marriage were perhaps intended for inclusion in the book on Pantisocracy he never got around to writing. One said: "On Marriage—in opposition to French Principles," and the other: "Marriage—sole Propriety in Paradise." Kathleen Coburn notes the close parallel of the second comment to Milton in *Paradise Lost*: "Hail wedded Love . . . / . . . sole proprietie,/In Paradise of all things common else."

Coleridge's concern that marriage be strictly preserved in Pantisocracy was shaped, and to a degree distorted, by his own experiences and attitudes. He recalled some years later that as a youth he had had "a short-lived Fit of Fears from sex," and the more unpleasant side of Coleridge's concern for Virtue and Duty is a puritanism that is closer to Bowdler than to Milton. During his 1794 walking tour, he twice remarked in letters on seeing people bathing naked. He did not disapprove, but he thought rather that "where sexual Distinctions are least observed, Men & women live together in the greatest purity. Concealment sets the Imagination a working, as it were, *cantharidizes* our desires." With the aid of a large dictionary we can infer that by this neologism he meant that concealment "poisons, makes bitter" the desires.

Having denounced Godwin's views on morality in his 1796 journal, *The Watchman*, he wrote a mutual friend that for him marriage was "that state in which it would be criminal to tempt to, or permit, an act of inconstancy." He then declared: "*Marriage is indissoluble.*" Marriage had its "moral uses" as well: "It is *Variety* that *cantharidizes us*. Marriage, that confines the appetite to one object, gradually causes them to be swallowed up in affection.

The most poignant demonstration of Coleridge's ideas on marriage was his own, to Sara Fricker. He had become engaged to her, to Southey's surprise and possibly to his own, in the fall of 1794. As William Haller has said, Southey entered Pantisocracy in order to get married, but Coleridge got married in order to enter Pantisocracy. He was at the time enamored of Mary Evans, whose family had befriended him during his school days in London. He wrote Mary that she was "possessed of a Mind and of a Heart above the usual Lot of Women," and when at the end of 1794 he realized that she was engaged to another, he wrote, "Southey! my ideal Standard of female Excellence rises not above that Woman. But all Things work together for Good. Had I been united to her, the Excess of my Affection would have effeminated my Intellect." He was *not* reconciled, however, to marrying Sara Fricker, and his explanation reflects his moralistic inhibitions concerning the sexual side of the marital relationship. "To marry a woman whom I do *not* love," he continued in the same letter to Southey, "to degrade her, whom I call my Wife, by making her the Instrument of low Desire," was a terrible thing to contemplate. Perhaps he would not even want her company when his "desultory Appetite" had been satisfied. Nevertheless, he promised, "*I will do my duty.*" Thus began a tragically mismatched marriage, one which Coleridge was unwilling to break because of his principles yet was unable to make anything more than a marriage in name only.

In theory, Coleridge believed in the equality of the sexes in Pantisocracy. In practice, he emphatically did not. He saw the women in the group as the potential spoilers of the system. They might never attain the strength of intellect and the liberal principles necessary. When Coleridge, in *The Watchman*, cited Tacitus approvingly concerning the women of ancient Germany, who were the equals of their husbands and their advisers on important issues, he was not thinking of Sara Fricker or of her mother. But he did find in Tacitus a support for his own notions. It was the "philosophy of sensuality," he agreed with Mary Woolstonecraft (the future Mrs. Godwin), to regret that the German women had abandoned the charms and wiles of femininity in becoming their husbands' companions. "What," he asked, "is this love which woman loses by becoming respectable?"

In a letter written to Southey after the widows Southey and Fricker had been added to the Pantisocrats, Coleridge described the role of the women in the commune. The two older women "can at least prepare the Food of Simplicity for us." Meanwhile "Let the married Women do only what is absolutely convenient and customary for pregnant Women or nurses—Let the Husbands do *all* the Rest," including "Washing with a Machine and cleaning the House." This would add no more than an hour's daily labor to the two or three hours necessary to live simply in the American wilderness.

One factor that had forced Coleridge into such mundane considerations was Southey's blithe proposal that two pairs of servants be taken with them into Pantisocracy. He was appalled at the idea, and endeavored to show both that servants were unnecessary and that such an inequality would preserve in Pantisocracy precisely the evils that afflicted contemporary civilization. Let the two couples join the group as equals, but not as servants. It was on this issue that Coleridge made a statement that expressed what for him was the principal reason that the communal experiment should be undertaken: "Wherever Men *can* be vicious, some *will* be. The leading Idea of Pantisocracy is to make men *necessarily* virtuous by removing all Motives to Evil—all possible Temptations." He was thinking here of the absolute social equality that must prevail within Pantisocracy. But the same principle applied to his views on the relations between the sexes. Only if the commune rested on a base of monogamous marriage would sexual desire develop into the higher passions of duty and familial responsibility.

It was also Coleridge's conviction that any sense of benevolence and philanthropy must begin quite literally at home. He entirely agreed with Godwin that all men were brothers and that benevolence should be universal; he entirely disagreed that therefore all less than universal affections should be discarded. In a letter to Southey he wrote that "The ardour of private Attachments makes Philanthropy a necessary *habit* of the Soul. . . . Some home-born Feeling is the *center* of the Ball, that, rolling on thro' Life collects and assimilates every congenial Affection." In the 1795 lectures, using a metaphor he may have borrowed from Pope's *Essay on Man*, he asserted that

> Jesus knew our Nature—and that expands like the circles of a Lake—the Love of our Friends, parents and neighbours leads us to the love of our Country to the love of all Mankind. The intensity of private attachment encourages, not prevents, universal philanthropy.

He contrasted this view to the "Stoical Morality" of Godwin, who mocking family ties and marital fidelity, "first adopts Principles so lax as to legalize the most impure gratifications, and then prides himself on acting up to his Principles."

It may be that Coleridge idealized family life, as family life would be in Pantisocracy, in part because of his unsatisfactory relations with his own family. He had been the spoiled youngest child of a large family, and after the death of his father, when he was ten, he seems not to have had much interest in or affection for any of his family save one brother. It never occurred to him to invite them to join him and the Southey *ménage* in America; they disapproved of his principles and he of theirs. In a series of autobiographical letters he wrote to Thomas Poole in 1797, he traced many of his psychological problems to his own childhood, when he was the lonely, spoiled little genius, hated by the other boys, pampered by old ladies, inept at all physical activity. Even after the dream of Pantisocracy had collapsed and he was settled with his wife and child at Nether Stowey, he was determined that it would be different for his children. They were to be raised from infancy "in the simplicity of peasants, their food, dress, and habits completely rustic." Coleridge would be their teacher. He himself at that time intended to learn the principles of agriculture from Poole, so that he could experience the same happy blend of physical and mental activity he had intended for Pantisocracy and now proposed for his children.

The same determination shapes one of Coleridge's finest poems, *Frost at Midnight*, written in 1798. Sitting beside his sleeping infant son, he recalls his own childhood in Devonshire and his school days in London. He tells the child that

> . . .thou shalt learn far other lore,
> And in far other scenes! For I was reared
> In the great city, pent 'mid cloisters dim,
> And saw nought lovely but the sky and stars.
> But *thou*, my babe! shalt wander like a breeze
> By lakes and sandy shores, beneath the crags
> Of ancient mountains, and beneath the clouds,
> Which image in their bulk both lakes and shores
> And mountain crags: so shalt thou see and hear
> The lovely shapes and sounds intelligible
> Of that eternal language, which thy God
> Utters, who from eternity doth teach
> Himself in all, and all things in himself.
> Great universal Teacher! he shall mould
> Thy spirit, and by giving make it ask.

Education, the second base upon which Pantisocracy was to have been built, was a topic that interested Coleridge all of his life. Before he decided instead to settle at Stowey, Coleridge considered an invitation to open a school at Derby, and it is reasonable to assume that the plans for that project were a continuation of the thoughts and conversations he had had on education during the year of planning Pantisocracy. Coleridge's notebooks for 1795-96 capture succinctly what for him should be the essence of education. In one entry he wrote: "What we *must* do, let us love to do. It is a noble Chemistry, that turns Necessity into Pleasure!" Another entry stated: "Unbiased mind—an absurdity."

The principal influences on his educational ideas were David Hartley and George Berkeley, the namesakes of his first two children. Hartley's *Observations on Man*, which had first appeared in 1749 and had been republished in the 1790's, was a particularly important influence. It was from Hartley, and also from his popularizer, Joseph Priestley, that Coleridge derived his doctrines of necessitarianism, which held that all human ideas and experiences moved inevitably toward an end of universal religiosity and benevolence, as ordained by a good God. Coleridge also agreed with them that everything that we are and know is the result of our experience. This led Coleridge to insist that the experiment of Pantisocracy would be complete only in the second generation, when the children of the founders had grown up in an environment purged of the corruptions of vice, wealth, and inequality.

It was because of his conviction that only education from infancy within the environment of Pantisocracy would produce beings truly free and freely virtuous that Coleridge wrote Southey with some asperity in October of 1794, after he had learned that Southey intended to take his family and all the rest of the Frickers with him into the wildnerness. He feared that this would be "subversive of *rational* Hopes of a permanent System," since the young Southeys and Frickers were already "*deeply* tinged with the prejudices and errors of Society." They had learned at school "*Fear* and *Selfishness*—of which the necessary offspring are Deceit, and desultory Hatred. *How* are we to prevent them from infecting the minds of *our* Children?" He assured Southey that he would accompany him even "on an *imperfect* system. But *must* our System be thus necessarily imperfect?"

In the same letter he expressed some doubts as to the capacity of their brides-to-be to understand the aims and ideals of Pantisocracy, and he therefore wondered "whether it is not probable, that the *Mothers* will tinge the Mind of the Infants with prejudications?"

It is clear from his letters of the Pantisocracy period that Coleridge then, as indeed throughout his life, believed that education was primarily moral. In this he sounds something like Rousseau in the *Emile*, who also believed that education meant less the accumulation of information than the acquisition of the moral habits and the sense of independence and responsibility that alone made one truly human. In one of his 1795 lectures, Coleridge wrote that while it was not difficult to understand that "vice is the effect of error and the offspring of surrounding circumstances," it was necessary that this perception be called "into action . . . in the daily and hourly occurrences of social life." Similarly, in a letter to Southey he wrote that it was easy to accept as an abstract proposition that the good of all and the good of each individual were identical, and that therefore it was each one's "*duty* to be Just, *because* it is his *Interest*." This was not enough: "The *Heart* should have *fed* upon the *truth*, as Insects on a Leaf."

In his next letter to Southey, he wondered if it would not be a good idea for all who intended to be members of "our Community" to be "incessantly meliorating their Tempers and elevating their Understandings?" It would also be desirable that the men master "a very respectable Quantity of *acquired* knowledge (History, Politics, above all, *Metaphysics*, without which no man *can* reason but with women & children)."

It was precisely this combination of "*acquired* knowledge" that Coleridge proposed as the curriculum of the school he thought of setting up in 1796. It would surely have been the curriculum in Pantisocracy. First, the pupils were to study "Man as Animal: including the complete knowledge of Anatomy, Chemistry, Mechanics & Optics." Then, "Man as an *Intellectual* Being," including the philosophical systems of Locke, Hartley, and the Scottish school, plus the new one of Kant. Finally, and clearly most importantly, they would consider "Man as a Religious Being," including a study of all religions. Then, moving from the individual to "the aggregate of Individuals & disregarding all chronology except that of mind," they would study the evolution of society, beginning with "Savage Tribes" and ending with "revolutionary states" and "Colonies."

Monogamous marriage and education were to provide the moral climate essential to an ideal society. The third base on which Pantisocracy was to rest, communism, would guarantee the absolute equality of all members of the society. Coleridge seemed to deny this tenet when he prefaced his recollections of Pantisocracy in *The Friend* with the statement that he had always held that "where property prevailed, property must be the grand basis of the government." It was not in fact a denial, however, since his 1795 writings make it clear that property would *not* prevail in Pantisocracy.

To Coleridge the abolition of property was only one aspect of Pantisocracy; true community would be achieved only when his ideas on marriage and family life and on education were fully worked out as well. For Southey, however, this aspect was central. Communism, at least as a rhetorical ideal, was something of an eighteenth century commonplace among the writers of the French Enlightenment and their Godwinian emulators in England. It was this different perception that may explain Southey's innocent transformation of the Pantisocratic project first into a good-sized emigration, then into what Coleridge aptly described as a "petty farming trade" in Wales. As a disciple of the republicans of ancient Rome and modern France, Southey certainly upheld stern virtue and marital fidelity, and Coleridge temporarily converted him to the psychological doctrines of Hartley. But in his letters and poetry of the period, the "pantisocratic" references are exclusively to a sort of automatic virtue that will appear once men live communally in the wilderness. He wrote in the first *Botany Bay Eclogue*, for example:

> ... Welcome, wilderness,
> Nature's domain! for here, as yet unknown
> The comforts and the crimes of polished life,
> Nature benignly gives to all enough,
> Denies to all a superfluity.

He looked forward, he wrote in a letter, to being able in America to "criticize poetry when hunting a buffalo and write sonnets whilst following the plough." He sounds remarkably like Fourier here, or like the young Marx, who wrote in *The German Ideology* that in communist society it would be possible for him "to hunt in the morning, fish in the afternoon, breed cattle in the evening, criticize after dinner, just as I like, without ever becoming a hunter, a fisherman, a herdsman, or a critic."[6]

Coleridge had an equally complete faith in the ability of a communal rural life to make men better, but as usual he expressed the idea in moral and Christian terms. He wrote a friend in 1796 that "the real source of inconstancy, depravity, & prostitution, is *Property*, which mixes with & poisons everything good—& is beyond doubt the Origin of all Evil." In the last of the *Lectures on Revealed Religion*, he added a similar twist to an argument he may have borrowed from Godwin's *Political Justice*. Godwin (and Coleridge) argued that most labor in modern society was in the production of superfluities and luxuries. If men worked only to produce what they really needed, and if this work were shared evenly, labor, Godwin concluded, would be "burthensome to none."[7] Coleridge's conclusion, on the other hand, was that thus "all of us might be learned from the advantages of opportunities, and innocent from the absence of Temptation."

The conclusion of his lecture stated, clearly and unequivocally, that in the Gospels Jesus prohibited his disciples from possessing property. The only permissible system was one of absolute economic equality: "As long as anyone possesses more than another, Luxury, Envy, Rapine, Government & Priesthood will be the necessary consequence, and prevent the Kingdom of God—that is the progressiveness of the moral World. . . . While I possess anything exclusively mine, the selfish Passions will have full play."

After 1795, Coleridge moved gradually away from the convictions of his youth, but the dream of Pantisocracy remained, if only as a fading ideal. It had been, after all, the greatest intellectual adventure of his youth. At the time that he first sensed Southey's lack of understanding of what the project meant to him, he wrote that "It is the Promethean Fire than animates my soul—and when *that* is gone, all *will be Darkness!*—I have DEVOTED myself!" Part of Pantisocracy's attraction for him, as I have suggested, was psychological. It offered the sense of purpose and of completeness that was missing in his relations with his family and in his life at Cambridge. There was perhaps a second reason that the project was so important to him. It should be remembered that the years of 1794 and 1795 called up in young English radicals a sense of anguish and a search for lost ideals not qualitatively different from that felt by young American radicals in 1972. England was in the midst of a divisive and profoundly unpopular foreign war. Worsening economic and social inequities brought not reform but massive indifference and a certain amount of repression. Many young radicals, including Southey and Coleridge, seriously believed that some sort of revolution was likely to occur soon in England. In the 1790's, this sense of frustration and despair was sometimes balanced by a belief that ultimately all would be well. For some this meant simply the triumph of the revolution; but for very many others the expected revolution was placed in a millenarian context. There had been a great surge of interest in the examination of biblical prophecy after the French Revolution began, in which the Bible was searched to see if contemporary events were not set out there as premonitions of the Second Coming of Christ. This was not merely the pastime of the ignorant masses. Isaac Newton, David Hartley, and Joseph Priestly had all taught that the Millennium could be inticipated by the interpretation of current events, and Hartley and Priestly had both contended that such interpretation indicated that it would come soon. In 1795, Coleridge shared this belief. In the long poem called *Religious Musings* he used Hartley's doctrines and the prophetic interpretation of current events to show that the Millennium was near at hand.

What is the connection of all this to Pantisocracy? First, the belief in the Millennium and the plan to establish an ideal community are perfectly compatible. John F. C. Harrison writes in his recent book *Quest for the New Moral World* that the ideas and plans of Robert Owen and his followers were products of a "culture" of millenarianism that was very widespread in England in the years around 1800.[7] Most and possibly all of the communities established in the United States in the eighteenth and nineteenth centuries held millenarian doctrines of one kind or another. Peter Mann, in his introduction to Coleridge's *Lectures on Revealed Religion*,[8] quite rightly sees millenarianism as the explanation of a passage in the first lecture in which Coleridge described "the small but glorious band":

> These are the men who have encouraged the sympathetic passions till they have become irresistible habits, and made their duty a necessary part of their self interest, by the long and continued cultivation of that moral taste which derives our most exquisite pleasures from the contemplation of possible perfection and proportionate pain from the perception of existing *depravation*.

He looked forward to "that glorious period when Justice shall have established the universal fraternity of Love." The possibility that he was thinking here of the Pantisocrats, who would be the instigators of the moral regeneration of mankind that would lead to the Millennium, is reinforced by his comment to Southey, after the latter's defection, that Southey had *"fallen back into the Ranks . . .* like the majority of men unable to resist a strong Temptation."

It is within this context, I think, that Coleridge's earlier declaration to Southey that "Pantisocracy is not the Question—it's realization is distant—perhaps a miraculous Millenium" should be understood. Coleridge had written in *Religious Musings* that Priestly had retired into the American wilderness where he "mused expectant on these promised years" of the reign of Jesus Christ. Coleridge himself had hoped to form a band of genuine Christians who, in that same wilderness, united by the bonds of community and family affection, would launch the moral regeneration of mankind that would precede the Millennium, the world-wide Pantisocracy.

As I said at the beginning, comparisons between the communes of the past and those of the present are of doubtful value. Yet perhaps Coleridge's ideas on Pantisocracy do offer some valuable insights for those who are thinking along similar lines today. He was surely correct, for example, in insisting that within a commune there was no feasible economic system except pure communism. With very few exceptions, those communal experiments that both prospered and persisted, such as the Shakers' settlements and the kibbutzim, were communistic.

In the second place, Coleridge was right to place such emphasis on education. There is a growing interest in "alternative education" as an adjunct of alternative societies, although not very many of the contemporary communes seem to have followed Coleridge in seeing that a different kind of society requires a different kind of education. And if Coleridge's ideas on education have little in common with those of Ivan Illich, both ask the question that any commune should surely ask: What is education *for*? In Coleridge's opinion, education should do what it has always tried to do. It should teach skills like writing and foreign languages and should instruct the child in his cultural heritage. Yet far more important, to his mind, was the development of the child into an autonomous moral person, freely virtuous because he is aware of the metaphysical and religious truths that lie behind superficial experience. To grow, to learn, meant to train and develop all of man's capacities, not simply his intellect. This sort of education is clearly impossible within the great society, but perhaps it *could* be tried in some contemporary pantisocracy in Oregon or Vermont. Such an education would probably benefit from being incorporated into communal child-rearing, an institution that Coleridge seems never to have considered.

Finally, what can be said for Coleridge's advocacy of what might be called "radical monogamy"? In the bulk of the contemporary communes, a Godwinian promiscuity, or at least sexual casualness, has been the norm. But Robert Houriet notes a number of communes in which couples have resumed monogamy, having found the other relationships too much of a hassle and marital fidelity worth the effort. If Coleridge's intellectualized and repressed conception of marriage were replaced by one that was free, passionate, and joyous, surely it would be possible to establish the sort of commune of which he dreamed, in which the bonds of marriage and family life led to a sense of community within the whole group that was genuine, deep, and lasting.

NOTES

1. All the quotations from Southey's letters are from Robert Southey, *New Letters*, ed. Kenneth Curry (New York, 1965).
2. Mrs. Henry Sandford, *Thomas Poole and his Friends* (London, 1888), I, 97-98.
3. Among the numerous studies of Pantisocracy I found these particularly helpful: Lewis Patton and Peter Mann, introduction to Samuel Coleridge, *Lectures 1795: On Politics and Religion* (Princeton, 1971); Carl R. Woodring, *Politics in the Poetry of Coleridge* (Madison, 1961), pp. 61-73; Jack Simmons, *Southey* (New Haven, 1947), pp. 38-58; Paul Kaufman, "New Light on Coleridge as an Undergraduate," *Review of English Literature* (Leeds), VII, 63-70; J. R. MacGillivray, "The Pantisocratic Scheme and its Immediate Background," in *Studies in English by Members of University College, Toronto* (Toronto, 1931), pp. 280-301; and Sister Eugenia, "Coleridge's Scheme of Pantisocracy and American Travel Accounts," *PMLA* XLV (1930), pp. 1069-84.
4. All quotations from Coleridge's writings are taken from the following: *Collected Letters*, ed. Earl Leslie Griggs (Oxford, 1956-   ); *Notebooks*, ed. Kathleen Coburn (New York, 1957-61); *Inquiring Spirit; a New Presentation of Coleridge from his Published and Unpublished Prose Writings*, ed. Kathleen Coburn (London, 1951); and the *Collected Works*, Kathleen Coburn general editor (Princeton, 1969-   ).
5. This approach coincides with that of Mann and Patton, introduction to *Lectures 1795*, and differs from that of the reviewer of *Lectures 1795* (E. P. Thompson?) in *Times Literary Supplement*, August 6, 1971, pp. 930-32.
6. Karl Marx, *Writings of the Young Marx on Philosophy and Society*, ed. Loyd D. Easton and Kurt H. Guddat (New York, 1967), p. 424.

7. Three recent books have been particularly significant in changing our understanding of English literary and cultural history during the period of the French Revolution: E. P. Thompson, *The Making of the English Working Class*, revised edition (Harmondsworth, 1968); Robert Erdman, *Blake: Prophet against Empire*, second revised edition (Princeton, 1969); and John F. C. Harrison, *Quest for a New Moral World* (New York, 1969).

8. Mann, introduction to *Lectures 1795*, p. lxxv. Lecture 1 was revised and published in 1795 under the title *A Moral and Political Lecture*.

A Word about *Soundings*

Since it began publication in 1968, *Soundings* has attracted a growing readership through its unique combination of scholarly competence and boldness. The list of authors published covers a wide spectrum of disciplines and levels of experience; it is not unusual for an issue to combine contributions from both established scholars and younger members of the academic community. In an era in which there is renewed concern for interdisciplinary discussion bridging the gaps between the natural sciences, the social sciences, and the humanities, *Soundings* has steadily promoted exchanges at a high level of competence and penetration.

Soundings publishes a special issue every year: last year's was on higher education, this year's is the present book, next year's will be entitled "The Rediscovery of Ethnicity: Its Implications for Culture and Politics in America." *Soundings'* regular issues have included articles by such authors as Michael Polanyi, Rosemary Ruether, Robert Bellah, and Michael Novak and articles on the economics and ethics of pollution control, pop architecture, sexual politics, Latin American political development, and the morality of new medical techniques.

The subscription rates for the journal provide a bargain for hardpressed scholars interested in interdisciplinary study. At $9 for one year, $15 for two, and $20 for three with student subscriptions at the reduced rate of $6, *Soundings* provides relevant and exciting input four times a year for the concerned reader. *Soundings'* address is P.O. Box 6309, Station B, Nashville, Tennessee 37235. The journal is sponsored by Vanderbilt University and the Society for Religion in Higher Education.

73 74 75   12 11 10 9 8 7 6 5 4 3 2